To Edwina
   in Friendship
      &
With happy memories
   of years in BaP together
      from
         Joy

         JJ

Chalk In My Hair

By Ivy Starkie

This book was written, designed
and published in 2011 by

Caroline Brannigan
1 Atkinson Avenue, Richmond,
North Yorkshire

www.carolinebrannigan.com
01748 821041

By carrying out extensive interviews, Caroline helps
clients to tell the story they have always meant to write

ISBN 978-0-9562965-9-7

Printed in the UK by the MPG Biddles Group
Bodmin and King's Lynn

*This book is dedicated to my late husband
John Starkie and to our son Tim, his
wife Maureen and their sons Stefan and
Andrew. It is also dedicated to the memory
of Philip Spencer, a young poet and RAF
officer killed during World War II.
Philip was my friend, my school love,
my mentor and my lover, without whose
influence my life and this ensuing story
would never have been written. May this be
my tribute to all like him who lost their
lives and their youth to a war.*

Thank you

To my family for their help in
compiling this book, to Peter Marshall
of BBC Television Manchester for
his programme about Burnley poet
Philip Spencer, to Philip's brother Ken
and Keith Whalley, whose reprint
of African Crocus, a book of Philip's
poems, began a revival of interest,
to Northern Life magazine and
Lancashire Newspapers for frequent
articles, to Lancashire Life for the
cover photograph, and finally to
memoir writer Caroline Brannigan.

Chapter One

On Pendle Hill

Few school children today know what a blackboard is, or have experienced the pride in being asked to clean its shiny surface or the thrill of hurling the chalk-laden blackboard rubber at their friends when teacher is out of the room.

Today everything is clean and on screen but when I taught, I grew accustomed to having chalk in my hair every day of my working life, for the dust got everywhere. Not only did I have chalk in my hair, I also had it in my blood, for my father was a teacher.

He taught me, I taught my son and later my daughter-in-law taught my grandsons. My Polish husband said he had to learn to speak good English or he wouldn't have got a word in edgewise with all these teachers around.

I was born in Padiham near Burnley, Lancashire, on February 21ˢᵗ 1922. My parents were Thomas and Ivy Starkie and I was named after my mother because I was born on her birthday.

When my mother was a teenager, there was no right to a full secondary education and many children had to leave school at 14 and go out to work. In Padiham that usually meant going into a cotton mill and that's what she had to do. In the 19th century, Burnley felt able to call itself the cotton weaving capital of the world. It was producing more cotton cloth than any other town and making more looms. But conditions for the workers, even in the early 20th century, were very tough, the air being full of cotton dust and the roar of the machines making speech impossible. My mother had to run six looms, three in front of her and three behind, and she couldn't cope with it.

Luckily for her, educational opportunities were expanding. After the opening of Padiham Technical School, my mother was able to leave the mill and study English, domestic science and home nursing. She was a brilliant pianist but women didn't get the opportunities they should have had in those days.

My father was a self-made man who was determined he wasn't going into the mill. In the First World War, he was in the Navy and after he came back he trained as a teacher. He became the science master at the technical school so he was able to support my mother after they married and she stayed at home to look after my sister Alice and me. Alice was six years older than I and of course she had done everything before me, so whatever she had done I had to do it too.

Life for me as a child seemed to be all school and chapel. Sunday was centred around the magnificent Wesleyan Chapel at the top of Padiham, built to hold a thousand. My father, who was a lay preacher, called it The Cathedral. My mother was in the choir.

Many of the women who attended services were weavers who had learned to lip-read against the roar of the looms. When my father was in the pulpit, he would sweep his eyes around the congregation and, if he spotted anyone having a

2

crafty lip-read gossip, he continued talking but fixed his eye on them until they were embarrassed into stopping.

I used that technique much later when I was called on to speak in public and found myself faced with 2,000 women. Gradually you get all the audience looking round to discover the object of your attention.

My father had a great spirit of public service and, as well as being a preacher, served on Padiham Urban District Council and later Clitheroe Rural District Council.

My father's father owned several houses in Hapton Road, Padiham, one of which became our home. An aunt and uncle lived next-door and my grandparents had another. When I was a toddler, my mother would say, "Go up as far as the lamppost and that's Grandma's" and off I'd go.

One day when I was quite small I heard a great noise outside and saw crowds of men marching up our hill. They were miners protesting at their low wages and that must have been during the General Strike in 1926. As a small child I had no idea of the dire conditions in which most of them lived and worked and looked nervously out of our front door at what to me was just a noisy rabble. "Don't go out there!" my father warned.

My grandfather was a very strict Methodist and the Lord's Day was absolutely sacrosanct. One day he came round and found me knitting on a Sunday and said, "You don't do that on the Sabbath!"

When I was about 10, my father retired and we moved out to Whalley. It is a lovely village four miles from Clitheroe. Our new house faced the main gateway to Whalley Abbey, the ruins of a 13th century Cistercian Monastery, a companion to Fountains Abbey. Monks always chose lovely places to live in, by a river on fertile land, and the

Ivy (front left), who had recently passed the 11-plus exam, with her parents and sister Alice in 1934. Alice was about to leave for teacher training college.

Abbey Lea, Whalley. Ivy and her family moved here after her father retired from teaching. It was her home from the age of 10 to 28. Ivy and her husband stayed in this house until their new home was ready and their son Tim was born here.

grounds became our park. My father took tourists round. Being in the land of the Lancashire witches, it was supposed to be haunted at night, though we never saw anything. Our house was on old abbey land and we often dug up glazed tiles from the abbey, clay pipes of the church wardens and pieces of stained glass.

It was out in the country and we thought we'd gone to heaven. After just one year at the local school, I did the wrong thing and won the Junior Scholarship. My name was mud afterwards, "That girl who's only been here five minutes!" The following year I started at Clitheroe Royal Grammar School. At 16 I did my school certificate and won a bursary to stay on for two years and take the higher certificate, a system now superseded by GCSEs and A-Levels.

When I wasn't working at my studies, my favourite walk as I grew into a teenager was to stride up the side of Pendle Hill, which sweeps dramatically to more than 1,800 feet. Standing panting at the summit, the cloud shadows racing across the slopes, I could see the Lancashire coast on a clear day. It's the kind of place that makes you feel good to be alive. When I go up Pendle Hill in my mind now, I am 17 again and I can forget for a moment the elderly lady's body in which I now, much to my surprise, find myself. I can't think how it happened!

To folks in the Ribble Valley, Pendle Hill is part of their lives and almost takes on a personality. It was customary to climb the lovely hill whenever we could.

They say that Pendle Hill is haunted. People have been going up there since the Bronze Age and probably before, so perhaps it is. For me it will always haunt me as the place I met Philip Spencer, to whom I became engaged. But I never became Mrs Spencer, for he was killed in 1943. Much later, I married my dear John, we had our son and I consider myself lucky to have been given a second chance at love by a good man. John had also suffered loss, so we understood each other. But I will never forget Philip.

We met at the top of the hill on August 15th 1939, and I believe it was fate. He'd come up from one side and I from the other, with cousins who were staying for a holiday. It was a perfect day. When we reached the beacon at the top, Mother produced her usual flask of tea and tomato sandwiches. The view was so clear, we could see almost to Blackpool.

Because Pendle couldn't quite stretch up to 2,000ft, my father encouraged us to pile up stones to make it a mountain. Suddenly, over the hill appeared this tall, good looking young man, with blond hair. I thought, "Ooh, he looks rather nice!" Was it coincidence or was it fate?

Philip and his family had set off from their home in Burnley for Philip to practise driving but he had tired of hauling the wheel around and on a whim he and his father decided to stretch their legs on Pendle, leaving his mother and two maiden aunts in a cafe.

In those days, young people were proud of their school blazers and wore them all the time. Seeing me in mine, Philip asked which school I was at and then revealed that he was a boarder at Richmond Grammar School in Yorkshire. He wasn't wearing his but instead looked very dashing and modern in a towelling T-shirt with a rope tie.

Sitting on the grass as the sun shone down, we chatted about school and the exams which were looming over us at the end of that academic year. The world looked so beautiful that day, it was impossible to believe in the storm clouds of war. We were young and therefore, of course, immortal. We spoke instead of literature and other subjects. Philip said, "I think it would be a good idea, don't you know," for that was how he spoke, a good Lancastrian lad, "if we got together and compared our ideas about our school work."

I wonder if 17-year-olds discuss exams when they first meet today? We had a bit of decorum then or perhaps we were a bit naïve. My school days were spent exclusively among girls and his among boys. He wanted to keep in touch and we agreed to write to each other, which surprised and rather thrilled me. When I asked him what he planned to do with his life he looked up dreamily and said he was thinking of taking holy orders. I shut up at that point. Holy orders? But he soon changed his mind about that!

So that was how it all started. I got a distinction in English Literature in my A-levels, and that was Philip's influence. I was doing the Lakeland poets and he was doing the Romantics and he'd be sticking up for Shelley and I'd be retaliating about Coleridge being on drugs.

A few days later Philip turned up at my home in Whalley bearing a photograph he'd taken on Pendle and with his mother in tow. I think she wanted to see this Ivy Starkie who had so captivated her son. They were cotton manufacturers and must have wondered if I was good enough. In turn I felt that my good education meant I could mix with anyone and I did. There was a great deal more inequality then but Mrs Spencer seemed to approve and became quite friendly with my parents.

Pendle Hill was always a special place for us, massive and rather mysterious. A curious atmosphere envelopes those who make it to the top. Its darkest story is of the so-called Witches of Pendle, 10 men and women found guilty of witchcraft in 1612 and hanged at Lancaster Jail. It was a time of superstition and mistrust and stories abounded that the accused had put spells on local people, resulting even in death. Even my own ancestors in the Starkie family were said to have believed the witches had put a spell on their children, though the symptoms described sound like epilepsy.

Both Philip and I were fascinated with the stories and, much later on, I wrote a thesis on Lancashire witchcraft. Being born in sight of Pendle, I qualify as a Lancashire witch and on being sent abroad later, one of the first books Philip packed to take with him was entitled The Lancashire Witches. In November 1939, to my delight, Philip sent me these lines in a letter:

> *There was a silence that was born*
> *A silence of rapture and joy*
> *A silence when two hearts have formed one love*
> *Of a girl and a boy.*

A romance of old Pendle between Ivy and Philip was born
when two 17-year-olds met on top of the hill

Chapter Two

Scarborough Blitz

In those brief moments that Philip and I had together, the rumblings of war had little reality for us. Even the Prime Minister's voice announcing soon afterwards on the radio that we were at war seemed something from another world. The streets were full of local young men striding off to join The Army, The Navy and The RAF but nothing would happen to us, we thought, for tragedy only happens to people you don't know.

We weren't prepared for what was to come. Meanwhile, term had started and Philip and I returned for our final year at school. Slowly my letters changed from "Dear Philip" to "My dear Philip". A Christmas reunion arrived at last and at New Year the Spencers held a big party at their home, to which I was invited with my mother and father. Their house was not very different from ours but they had a resident housekeeper, and I thought, There's posh! When you wanted something you just sat in your chair, rang the bell and in came Margaret. I wished I had one.

Yet there was never any question of snobbery and their welcome was warm, if rather prim and proper. In return I played some carols on their piano. There was a kiss for me from Philip under the mistletoe and we both knew things were becoming more serious between us. With the so-called phoney war going on in the background, when the horrors stayed mainly at sea, we buried our heads in our books, our letters and our application forms, in my case for teacher training college and, for Philip, to St. John's College, Oxford.

In my sixth form, we were all trying to decide what careers we could do. There weren't many professional opportunities for women, it was Civil Service, nursing or teaching. Most parents wouldn't pay for their daughters to go to university or medical school because it was expected that when you married, you'd give up work. In some jobs that was compulsory. Lots of colleges wouldn't even consider women. I got a scholarship to teacher training college, which helped towards the costs but it wasn't free.

I had a good friend and I can see her now, sitting on the desk with her feet on the chair, announcing, "I'm going to go to university to train in economics." And she did, later on going into politics and becoming well known as Dame Judith Hart, Minister for Overseas Development. She had it all worked out, even at 18.

My sister Alice did her teacher training at Bingley, Yorkshire, and visiting her all-female college left me distinctly unimpressed as they were obliged to wear whistles round their necks even when walking in the college grounds in case they were molested.

When my turn came to choose a college, I disregarded my father's advice to follow Alice to Bingley and instead, with three friends from school, joined the City of Leeds Training College, a co-educational establishment, in 1940.

But I never went to Leeds as in 1939, when World War II broke out, the college building was taken over as an emergency hospital to cope with the expected casualties. Students were moved to Scarborough where hotels now devoid of tourists were taken over as hostels and, at times, classrooms.

You couldn't call it an evacuation exactly because Scarborough was far from safe. Being a harbour town and later on a training centre for thousands of RAF aircrew, we were bombed practically every night. But there were empty buildings available there for the college to use and so we had to put up with it.

Arriving at the station, we were met by students calling out the names of the hotels to which we had been allocated. Mine was The Dorchester. Being Starkie and, as usual, nearly last on the list alphabetically, I had a room right at the top which meant a lot of stairs to haul up, or rush down when the air-raid siren went.

Being catapulted from a fairly sheltered, chapel-led life into the exciting atmosphere of a seaside town packed with young men and women was a great eye-opener to me. Originally I had applied to Leeds because I had a Starkie uncle living in Headlingley who my father thought would keep an eye on me. That's just how things were then for women.

Despite the danger, my two years in Scarborough were great fun because we were young and all in it together. You made friends with air crew knowing they could be killed once sent to their bases but you couldn't think too much about it. That was the only way to get through. Life expectancy for a pilot in a dog fight was 20 minutes!

I remember when they first arrived. I returned to Scarborough after a half-term at home to find the hotel almost deserted. "Where is everyone? What's happened?"

I asked and heard that 3,000 air crew had descended on the town and everyone had rushed off to see this phenomenon in Air Force blue.

From then on our social life moved up a gear. I don't think the college really liked the idea of fraternising but what could they do? I had to study navigation as part of my geography course and so we would say we were going up to a hill called Oliver's Mount to study navigation, only of course our 'instructors' were the RAF.

They were lovely boys. Miss Wood used to lecture us about being careful with "these older men" but they weren't, most were the same age as us. They wanted to live it up because life expectancy once on active service was so short.

So I had many friends who were boys but my heart was in Oxford where Philip was now studying English Literature. He had been writing poetry since he was 11 but it wasn't until we had been together for some time that he started showing me his poems, sending them by post to me in Scarborough.

Sheaves of typewritten sheets would arrive. They weren't all good, the outpourings of first a boy, then a young man, but some were beautiful and showed promise of depths as yet unplumbed. These eventually appeared in a volume entitled *The First Hundred*.

You can see quite clearly the influence of the land in which he grew up and his love of Nature and the environment. To me, his poems were just like him talking. The romance of Pendle Hill is there. At that point he didn't say a lot about me in his poetry but he spoke of the places which were special to us. As time went on, scenes of punting and cream cakes crept into his poetry, typical of his life in Oxford.

At Oxford Philip studied in an exalted group of

Ivy Starkie 1942

Trainee teachers in Scarborough 1940/41. See Ivy, below.

14

undergraduates including Philip Larkin and Kingsley Amis and his talents were blossoming. He loved Oxford, immersed in a world of words, but war was waiting outside the study door, impatient to pluck him away.

Like most young people then, we made the most of the time we had together during the holidays, walking and talking and delighting at being in love.

During our long separations, the letters flew between us like arrows. Phoning usually was out of the question - too expensive, confined to chilly phone boxes and cut short by operators anxious to keep lines clear for war matters.

Paper became scarce and Philip went scrounging round for anything to write on, even on one occasion sheets of Izal, a hard, translucent toilet paper. Another time I got half a paper table cloth. Sometimes it would all be in Latin, simple stuff like "time flies" and "I've a lot to do" and I wondered, who else is getting letters in Latin? I'll have to keep on my toes with this young man! But it felt good to have my intellect stretched in this way.

I still had my copy of my school poetry book, Palgrave's Golden Treasury. Sometimes Philip would write to me and tell me, if he didn't have time to write a poem of his own, to turn to a particular page and "read a poem with me". We were never without poetry between us. One was called To Lucasta, Going to the Wars, which begins,

Tell me not, Sweet, I am unkind
That from the nunnery
Of thy chaste breast and quiet mind
To war and arms I fly.

And there was Shakespeare's sonnet 116:

Let me not to the marriage of true minds
Admit impediments. Love is not love
Which alters when it alteration finds

Philip wasn't always scribbling. One day he climbed out on to the college roof and put his pipe into the mouth of a gargoyle. Despite being a generally serious boy, he had a sense of humour and we'd never have got on without that because I like to have a joke. In November 1942, by then far away, Philip looked back to his university days with fondness and wrote this poem:

Those We Had Known

We used to talk of those we had known
Who had gone down:
Some made us laugh
Others were cynics and we despised them:
Some were merely affectatious and we knew, like the seed, soon
they would wither away:
We talked about them as we drifted along in a punt,
May-flies swarming over us, the still water, and the summer
afternoon was cool beneath the star-shade of elms.
As we lazed in the boat George made occasional deep plunges
with the puntpole,
And a corner of the Cherwell brought Magdalen Bridge in
sight.
We talked of them over beans on toast and iced fruit tart in a

small restaurant in George Street,

Or over patties in the Cadena if we felt elite.

We talked about them at nights when we strolled about the gardens after Hall, swinging our gowns,

When the siren had blown and the only light came from the stars and the full moon which shone on the smooth roofs and spires in the South-East.

We talked about them over tea,

When we brought them into our small rooms to eat with us,

Or when they came uninvited, hearing the rattle of teacups, and a kettle falling.

We talked about them as we cycled to hockey

And when we wandered to Whytham

And stopped at the Trout to drink, and admire the peacocks,

And the deep waters of the Isis swirling under Godstow Bridge.

We talked of them when there were three of us together

In the days of our happiest friendships.

We had just outlived the names of freshers when we went down.

Behind we left friends.

Who had had tea with us,

Punted with us.

Knew Isis and the Cherwell and Godstow Bridge

They had shared our delights,

And now that we are gone,

Will they think of us –

What will they think of us?

Those We had Known was published in African Crocus, a collection of poetry by Philip Spencer, Fortune Press, 1954.

Philip and I both enjoyed our student days, though we were far apart. In my crowd at Scarborough, nobody had much money, so it was mainly long walks and maybe fish and chips. We girls were clock watching all the time because we were supposed to be back at the hostel by 10 o'clock. Some of the girls were real tinkers and used to escape again, though I didn't. I still went to church every Sunday and was in the choir.

There were always little parties going on in our rooms at the hotel, though that was strictly girls only and just tea or coffee and a few snacks, for it was hard to get many treats because of all the food shortages. Our parents would send parcels of goodies which we'd share. We had very little cash. All meals were provided. You were expected to have a Post Office savings book containing enough money for your fare home and a few pence left over to spend. Can you imagine it? They'd go mad today.

By being very careful with our pennies, my friend and I would have enough on a Saturday to go down to Rowntrees, the smart department store, where the door would be opened for us and we swept in feeling very grand. In the café we could just about afford coffee and waffles. That was marvellous, for we were always hungry.

By this time my sister Alice was teaching in Manchester and was being bombed there. I was being bombed in Scarborough and our parents were pleasantly ticking on in rural Whalley. Despite our village being a relatively safe area, we had made the recommended preparations at home, putting strips of sticky paper across the windows to limit flying glass and, being artistic, I'd done all sorts of pretty patterns.

We were bombed only once in Whalley and that must have been because I had come home for Christmas, hoping for a rest from all the raids and disturbed nights. They were out to get me, or so it seemed. In fact they were aiming for a railway viaduct but missed.

I'd gone to the cinema with a friend. Suddenly, a bomber flew over and dropped a stick of bombs somewhere. My friend, a lad who was in the LDV, Local Defence Volunteers, who were later renamed the Home Guard, jumped up from his seat and shouted, "Don't panic! Don't panic!" I have to laugh now because it was just like Corporal Jones in the television show Dad's Army. He had no idea what to do because he'd never been in a raid before. For me, it was normal. The air-raid siren had in fact sounded only after it was all over.

When I arrived home, I discovered that two bombs had fallen in a field behind our house, so we had a lucky escape. Two others had fallen on the other side of the viaduct. I found my father surveying the chaos in his garage after the bomb blast had shattered every bottle stored there.

The story later was that the bomber, possibly on its way home from some much bigger attack, had spotted a train standing in Whalley Station with the light shining from its firebox. It was a sitting target but they didn't get it.

During my teacher training, lectures would be held occasionally at the hotel which served as our hostel but most of the classes were held at Scarborough College, a boys' school. We had to keep up standards, which was good, and discipline was never dropped at all, no matter how bad the conditions. We had to be on time for class even if we had spent the whole night in the shelter, which was in the hotel's reinforced cellar, and crunched our way over broken glass to reach the college. What stays in my mind most from The Blitz is the sound of broken glass tinkling everywhere.

Bathtime was by rota and about three days after I'd arrived, I'd just got in mine at about six o'clock when the siren went. Everyone else was rushing down to the shelter and banging on the bathroom door telling me to get a move on. Stepping out, I dried myself as best I could but pulling on clothes over damp skin took an agonising age, the sound of approaching planes adding to the tension.

Thick blackout curtains secured firmly at the edges were put up by the hotel maids before they went off duty, which was cosy in winter but in summer meant you were sealed in from about six.

I studied art as part of the course and one evening I had just spread out my paper and paints when the hostel warden, Dolly Wood, put her head round the door and told me to look out of the window. Right behind us was a hill called Oliver's Mount and the whole area was covered with blazing incendiary bombs. We'd never seen that before.

"What do you think's going to happen?" asked Miss Wood, nervously.

"I think it means they're going to come!" I answered, and sure enough they did. That became the pattern, incendiary bombs to light up the targets followed by the big stuff from the heavy bombers.

They usually came over about teatime and sometimes the siren would go as I was out playing my violin during music practice with the orchestra and we had to either find a shelter or risk trying to get back. I suppose we were scared but we were all in it together and that helped. The worst night was in March 1941 when, huddling in the hotel cellar, we heard a huge explosion close by. Queen Margaret's School opposite had been shattered by a parachute mine and, although the building was empty at the time, it claimed the life of one of our students who was walking past.

Gazing up at the sky, he saw what he thought was an enemy airman floating down on a parachute but instead it was a bomb, designed to cause maximum devastation. He died later from his injuries.

This lad had played the double bass and sparkled at our dances where he would pluck the strings and spin it round. It was very difficult to accept that he was now dead.

The hotel owner was Mr Thompson - we used to call him ITMA after the radio show It's That Man Again. After the explosion he ventured out and came back clutching a mass of green silk which turned out to be the parachute from the mine which had blown into the hotel entrance.

That night, after the all-clear had sounded, I returned to my room with the two girls who shared it to find all the windows blown out and many of our things shattered. Photo frames lay in pieces on our three dressing tables, the mirrors had cracked and glass and plaster covered our beds.

To cheer ourselves up, we opened a parcel which one of the girls had received from home and shared out the contents. Suddenly there was a knock on the door. It was an official to assess the bomb damage and there we were munching away amid the devastation as if nothing had happened.

We had to take our turn at fire-watching, which meant slapping on a tin helmet and patrolling outside the hotel looking for incendiary bombs. These, though small, could spark an inferno if not doused quickly. To do this we formed teams to operate a stirrup pump, one pumping, one filling the buckets of water to feed it and another directing the hose.

Fire-watching was pretty dramatic stuff, with the crump, crump of bombs dropping, the roar of planes, the boom of our anti-aircraft guns and shrapnel raining down. Sometimes soldiers would go past and tell us to get inside as they thought it was getting too dangerous for young girls to be out.

Our families at home only knew we were alright when they got our letters, for few of them had telephones to receive an instant message of reassurance.

Fire drill was taken in deadly earnest and we all had to be out in two minutes, which was quite something when you had to clamber down the fire escape from the top floor, as I did. One girl froze completely with vertigo and couldn't budge. There was the warden Miss Wood yelling at us to get down and I was blinding away at this girl. In the end I got her to face the wall with me behind her and somehow we edged down together.

One morning I awoke to find one of the male students looking dishevelled on our doorstep. His hostel, Villa Esplanade, had had a direct hit. All had survived but had only the clothes they stood up in, so I lent him my jumper. It was a revelation to me because there were we girls, rushing obediently to the shelter, taking with us a bag kept permanently packed with essentials, and here were the men not bothering with a shelter at all, let alone a bag. They were lucky the bomb hit an empty part of their hotel. Later, the lad's mother sent me a cake to thank me.

As well as my little bag, when the siren went I'd grab my

silky, slippery eiderdown to sleep on in the shelter and one night, rushing down, it slid from my hands, tumbled down the stairs and everyone else went slithering down over it, so I wasn't very popular.

My mother, being a Lancashire woman, put every scrap of news she had in her letters, even going up the sides when the page ran out, for paper was scarce. To take our minds off the danger, Miss Wood would say as we huddled in our shelter, "Ivy, have you had a letter from your mother?" and get me to read it out.

There would be demands about whether I had my winter woollies on, which brought hoots of laughter for we were more worried about being blown to pieces.

Winters on that East Coast could be wickedly cold. PE was held every day in the grounds of Scarborough College, in shorts whatever the weather, and I've never been so frozen. I came to the conclusion that the best way to play hockey was to run up and down to stay warm but keep out of the way of the ball as much as possible.

The idea was to train us to teach PE and every now and again I'd be made referee. To show willing, I'd blow my whistle from time to time. "What are you blowing the whistle for, Miss Starkie?" they'd want to know and I'd have to think fast and come up with something about being over the line. I could not see what hockey, forward rolls or anything like that were going to do for me in life.

Teaching practice was at Hinderwell Primary School and we all began to think about jobs. I decided I couldn't face infants, all those kids with faulty plumbing. I wanted to work with an older age group and really get them somewhere.

Chapter Three

The Last Goodbye

Meanwhile, the cold fingers of war were creeping round the peaceful Oxford colleges where students were now forced to take a shortened war degree of only 18 months so they could join the fight against tyranny.

Naturally we were all still thinking about the long-term future, though we didn't know who would have one and who wouldn't. Philip was a keen photographer. He wanted to go into films and spent his holidays hovering around Pinewood Studios near London. I wonder what we might have seen on our screens if he had been able to do so for his poetry extended from the page to his eye. He made cine films and showed them to family and friends in a spare bedroom converted by his mother into a home cinema.

I never saw Philip in Oxford and he never came to Scarborough. It would be a tortuous cross-country train journey today and in overcrowded wartime conditions was near impossible. Petrol for private cars was nonexistent and posters asked us if our journey was really necessary. So we met only at home in the holidays.

In early 1942 Philip volunteered for the RAF. He would have been called up anyway. Had he been at university in

Philip Seafield-Grant Spencer, B.A. (Oxon)
volunteers to join the RAF

the North, he would have been sent to Scarborough but from Oxford he was directed South. Fate had brought us together but now it seemed determined to keep us apart.

We had no idea how little time we had left together. In the early summer he was given embarkation leave before being sent overseas and went home to say goodbye to his family and mine. Despite being in love, Philip and I had always been very sensible people and there are times when I wish we had been a bit more impulsive for I might have seen him one more time.

I was deep into final exams but had completed everything important with only art to go. Philip asked my mother not to tell me he was home. "She's doing her finals and they're important to her," he told my mother. In my hostel at Scarborough, I opened a letter from her to say that Philip had been - and gone. I think she should have told me he was home but how could she go against Philip's wishes? I'd have ditched the art exam and scrambled back as quickly as possible.

The last time I spoke to Philip was on the phone to West Kirby near Liverpool where he was waiting with hundreds like him for a boat to take him far away. His thick, woollen uniform had been replaced by tropical kit, so we knew he was going somewhere hot. But where? From West Kirby he wrote a letter in which he pledged his commitment to me, adding. "I won't break that. We will be together as soon as I come home." And so we became engaged. There was no romantic proposal on Pendle Hill, as we might have preferred, and no ring but the commitment on each side was no less strong for that. How unkind of fate to arrange that we couldn't even kiss each other goodbye.

As well as being separated from Philip, I also had to cope

with being parted from most of my Scarborough friends who had been flung to the four winds. My bedroom at home felt strange without other girls to share it.

In September 1942 I started work at a primary school in Higham, right under Pendle Hill. The sweeping slopes were both a comfort and an agony of memory for me. Philip wrote from the troop ship but letters took six weeks to reach me and it was a long time before I could even try to visualise him in his new, alien environment, so different from the one outside my window.

"I know I'm going to be in trouble here," he wrote from the crowded deck, feeling the sun grow hotter each day as they ploughed ever southwards. "It's not my world, please keep on writing, your letters are such a treat, the jolliest and longest I ever had." He also said I ought to write a book. It's taken a while but I have at the age of 88.

The troop ship set off from Liverpool, then sailed at first north up the Scottish coast before eventually heading south, to avoid the most dangerous routes. As temperatures rose on the overcrowded ship, Philip slept on deck. By day he pored over his poems, a finger caressing his stubbly chin, for water was too precious for shaving. When he looked up he saw flying fishes skimming across the waves and hoped nothing more sinister was lurking in the form of a German U-boat. In one letter he wrote, "I have a friend sitting next to me who says I have a good look on my face and that's because I'm writing to you, Ivy."

In another from the ship he noted that the date was August 15th 1942, three years since the day we had met on Pendle Hill. "I'm going to write a few lines about the occasion of our meeting," he went on and there was a short poem for me:

Three years ago you were to me unknown
Yet when another hour rolls by
You and I to each other shall be sure
No longer shall I trudge my life alone
And wander on, not knowing why, aimlessly
No smiles, perchance a moan.

But then, rejuvenated with a guide
To follow and a queen to attend
With a friend
Whatever may betide
Then Cythne love, my intellectual bride
Though fate may for your layon send
To the end, we shall go smiling, side by side.

(He noted, "Not much to show for half an hour's work. Please accept and consider it not from its poetic defects but for the spirit and feeling. Please be exceptionally tolerant, as only you can be.")

I have included extracts from letters and copies of the originals to illustrate the tragedy of separation endured by millions during the war.

When I addressed my envelopes to Leading Aircraftsman Philip Spencer, there was only a Forces postal number to direct my words to him and it was a long time before I found out where he was. Philip, disembarking in a stream of young men, found himself in Rhodesia, now Zimbabwe. A stack of my letters, which had gone by air, awaited him.

So great had been the slaughter among RAF crews that

The letter containing a poem written for Ivy on the anniversary of her first meeting with Philip on Pendle Hill

Britain couldn't train new ones quickly enough and young men were sent to the colonies, including Canada, Rhodesia and South Africa, to learn their skills.

Later, when Philip was moved to South Africa, I suggested he nip into De Beers, the diamond jewellers, and pick up something to make into an engagement ring for me. I knew he couldn't afford a big diamond and wrote, "Just pick up some chips, bring them home and we'll make a ring when you get back." The material aspects of a ring meant nothing to me. I wasn't interested in flashing it under people's noses. But it would have been a comfort to me to have worn Philip's ring to show everyone what we meant to each other.

Some young men adored the thrills of the RAF but to Philip's more artistic soul, the endless studying of technical skills to become a navigator were a drudgery. I sent books on philosophy to take his mind off the daily routine and tried to picture him stooped over his notebook, composing poems of the new land in which he found himself.

Philip's earlier poetry was the product of what he had been then, a schoolboy just feeling his strength, but now his work was maturing from boy to man. Here is an example, composed amid the humdrum daily life of training and inspections.

Disenchantment was written during inspection in Moffat, Rhodesia (now Zimbabwe) April 5th 1943 and sent to me on a page torn from his notebook.

Disenchantment (written specially for Ivy)

If they could see you now –
Those whose kisses still taste upon our lips.
Still poising as they did at the parting
Which led us here,
Unwilling, -
Those who are proud of us
Thinking we fight like tomorrow's headlines.
They will open their Mirror – or their Times –
And see stories of a river of Russian blood,
And hostage-slaughter of a hundred gallant slaves
In a tiny land.

They imagine they can see us,
They think of us,
Are proud of us serving with these our brothers who fall
Screaming in their red sunset death,
The mad unnatural serenade to God.
Yes, we are the living comrades of these dying brothers,
We, immaculately disciplined in life as they in death,
Not by their sides,
Bleeding with their bleeding, broken with their pieces, -
We, shining in Silvo, Cherry Blossom soldiers,
Standing by our beds for barrack-room inspection,
While those kisses still linger on our lips.

Though Philip wasn't one of the wild ones, he was no saint. One letter listed, "Breakfast - one aspirin. Lunch - one aspirin. Dinner - one aspirin" and I knew he'd been on a blinder, so he did let off steam now and then. As well as his aircrew studies, somehow he found time to write both poetry and prose. Despite having officially graduated from a shortened wartime course, he knew 18 months had been snatched from him and was longing to return to Oxford to do a Masters degree.

He had done one thesis on Shelley and now, finding himself in a world of racial inequality and disharmony, he wrote another on apartheid, which would become official policy a few years later. Travelling by bus, he was appalled to see black people sent to the back of the queue in preference to whites, so he joined them.

I supported his moral courage but was frightened to death that he'd be shot by some of the extremist whites who backed this ludicrous regime but Philip insisted, "If I wait for a bus, I wait in my right place." All that upset him very much. A keen photographer, he tried to photograph the black people he met but was stopped by whites.

In the rising heat and dust of the Southern Hemisphere's early summer, Philip longed for the cool breezes of Lancashire. I told him I had taken my pupils for a walk along Cow Lane at the foot of Pendle and in one of his last letters to me, he wrote, "How lovely to read about Cow Lane in the heat of South Africa!"

I had a book of folk songs which I often played and sang for Philip and he took a copy with him, including Old Pendle:

Pendle, old Pendle, by moorland and fell
In glory and loveliness, ever to dwell
On life's faithful journey, where e'er I may be,
I'll pause in my labours, and oft think of thee.

In the following extract from a poem he called The Music of Names and which he dedicated to his brother Ken "because it is about times we shared", he looks back to the landscape which inspired him. It was written on March 19th 1943:

Towneley is dark with thick oaks,
and the ash trees' leaves are falling,
Mention but Pendle and the winds and the curlews would come,
Speak then of Hambledon - it is like myself that is calling,
Whisper but Burnley and my soul with my thoughts goes winging home.

He was, nevertheless, able to appreciate the beauty of his natural surroundings. Writing in his poem Sentinel in July 1943, sitting on Shelly Beach at East London, South Africa, he recorded,

An endless night,
An endless sea,
But a timeless moon,
Companion to my solitude.

I know now that Philip had always sensed he would not see England again. Knowing he was not yet even in the theatre of war, I had no such qualms and continued my daily life as best I could. I was working at the village school at Higham, which wasn't that far from home but my journey involved two buses which never waited for each other, so I was always behind times.

On December 1st 1943, I had taken my first bus from Whalley to Padiham and was waiting for the connection to Higham. In my bag was a half-finished letter to Philip. The only sign of war was the queue snaking out of the fishmonger's where shoppers hoped for an unrationed boost to their monotonous meals. Trotting from the queue came a woman who was a mutual friend of the Spencers. She sat down beside me on the bus and said, "Have you heard about Philip?".

"Is he home?" I asked, hopefully, knowing he should soon be on his way.

"No, he's been killed," she said.

Can you imagine getting a bombshell like that? "But I'm just writing him a letter," I stammered. What daft things you say in shock.

Stunned and disbelieving, I arrived at school like an automaton and worked all day. My headmistress was a serious woman who always arrived wearing a large, formal hat. She saw me looking as white as a sheet and asked me if I was alright, so I told her. She was kind in her way but not as kind as I would have been to someone who had just walked in and said their fiancé had been killed.

She thought I should do my day's work but didn't want me to be alone during the break, for I probably would have broken down then. As we drank our coffee together, we heard the news headlines on the radio, "Eight of our bombers are missing." I knew that wasn't Philip but in my head did the arithmetic: eight crews of eight, that's 64 losses. It was dreadful. I just thought, "Where is God?"

This was a foretaste of what was to come, to put up and shut up, to be expected to carry on, to hide grief for fear that the huge burden of sadness carried by so many bereaved souls would sink the country's morale. Decorum swamped our natural feelings. Today there would be hysterics and counselling, which is more human.

At the end of the day there were two buses to take and then I was stepping through the back door to the familiar Wednesday smell of baking. At last I broke down. My mother had already heard the news and said, "We weren't going to tell you until you'd had your meal." She probably wanted to feed me up before the shock. I went upstairs and laid on the bed and howled. The next morning I got up, bathed my eyes and went to work. I never missed a day but at night, alone in my room, I cried for weeks.

Philip had been killed on November 25th 1943 in a training accident in South Africa. After his plane hit a pine tree in a forest, he was pulled from the wreckage and taken to a house in the forest where he died the following day. He was 21.

The Spencers had received a telegram soon after and were in deep shock. We had no phone at home, so they couldn't ring me. They had written to my home, of course, but the news found me first.

His mother was absolutely devastated and I don't blame her at all but I do blame the system by which fiancées and girlfriends were completely excluded by officialdom from the direct news and aftermath of the death of their loved one. I felt very left out of it all, with no say in his memorial service or any say on where his few belongings went. I would love to have had his diaries but those went elsewhere. He must have kept my letters to him but what happened to those? Not being a widow, I had no claim on Philip, as far as most people were concerned.

I felt very much on the outside. The memorial service was conducted at St. Peter's Church, Burnley by the Bishop but I remember hardly a thing about it. A carved wooden screen now stands there to commemorate Philip's short life, commissioned by his family.

Later, Philip's things arrived and his mother asked me to look at them with her. I saw this one suitcase in his bedroom, almost his whole short life packed up inside it, and it broke my heart. In the wardrobe hung his civilian clothes, as if he would walk in at any moment. I could have gone in there and hugged them. Philip had written from the troopship and called me his 'intellectual bride' but we were denied the chance of married life.

I discovered that Philip had believed he would die and had written to his younger brother Ken to say so: "I shall die but you will still see me." To me he had said only that I was to ensure his poetry was published but even that went out of my hands.

Philip's mother was very much a woman of her time who felt that I was young and that the best thing for me was to try to forget. People kept saying to me, time will heal. But time does not heal and I felt they all lied.

Adding to my sense of isolation was the fact that none of my friends had known him and had no shared memory. My parents and his knew we had a commitment but it wasn't widely acknowledged. By now my sister Alice was married and her husband, who had been stationed in South Africa and India, returned home. That was hard, though I was glad for them. Somehow I clung to my Christian faith, even through the most poignant lines of the hymns we sang. "Those far distant need thy care," I sang, wondering, "but He hasn't, has He?" I was angry with God.

I couldn't show my feelings. Nobody did. People all over were losing their loved ones. You were just expected to get on with your life. Attitudes were very different then. Hardest of all was hearing a letter from him drop on to the doormat, as if his death was just a bad dream. The time lag for deliveries from South Africa was so long that this agony went on for six weeks.

One of his last letters to me was written on the beach at Grahamstown, where he watched the pine trees in the distance. They seemed to haunt him. As his ship had sailed from England, it was the pine trees on the hills which he longed for, and it was in a pine forest that he met his death. His very last letter was dated November 16th 1943, when his course had almost finished and he expected to be posted, hoping it would be Britain. We had both thought a reunion was only a few weeks away.

Philip is buried with his crew in East London, Cape Province, South Africa. Photographs of the funeral were sent to his family. I only know where he lies because a friend, who lives in East London, went up to the cemetery and sent me photographs of his grave, which is up on a hillside. It's a great sadness to me that his gravestone is inscribed, Leading Aircraftman, when it should have read, Flying Officer, for he had just received his commission. Each year, through the Royal British Legion, I send a poppy wreath to his grave but I have never been there. At first war and its aftermath prevented travel and by the time it would have been possible, fate had brought me a second chance of happiness.

The Evelyn Valley Forest Station to which Philip was taken after the crash and where he died

Written on a page torn from Philip's notebook on the beach at Grahamstown, November 1943.

My sweetest one

Be this the shortest note I ever write, I must write it now. I have found the pinewoods again - and I shall thank Grahamstown for ever and ever for it. As we left Scotland, the wind carried the scent of the pines down to the boat for one delicious moment - it was England's own farewell to me. And now I have found the message of the pines again. Here I am, among the pine trees, alone, and yet far from being alone.

For all these trees, and the wind washing among them, are my friends and you are here and all that was ever beautiful and good and true - all that I ever loved in England from my childhood days upward, all are gathered around me now, only a little less lovely than their real selves while they must remain beneath their veil of thoughts.

Here, beneath a loveliness almost English, white clouds and blue sky, treetops and a bird singing, I think I have found true happiness, and perhaps I have found God.

My love goes with you always, my darling, my dearest one, Phil

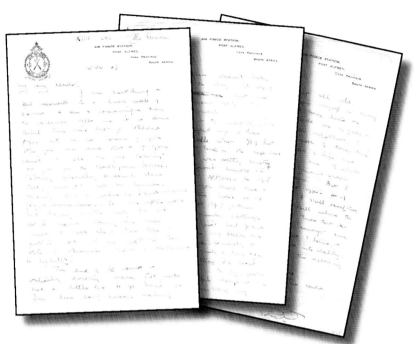

*Philip's last letter 16ᵗʰ November 1943, received six
weeks after he was killed. This was dreadful for Ivy
to bear, knowing that Philip was dead.*

My very dearest,

*I am snatching a few moments of a very busy week of exams
to pen a communiqué since the calendar tells me it is some
awful time since last I stabbed paper with pen in honour
of you. Hope you can read this - if you can't, it will be good
training for you for the Intelligence Service. Nothing directly
personal about that. And it's not an opinion.* (He thought I'd
be good in Intelligence).

*Having done a paper on reconnaissance this afternoon and
having written away for two solid hours, having ten times
more to talk about than time to put it into, I am not in the
state of steadiness which is conducive to legibility. The end*

of the course is rapidly drawing near. Two weeks and a little bit to go. Mind you, I have been long enough reaching this point and there haven't been any flowers on the way. It wasn't uphill going but just a long, monotonous trek. The hills are ahead now.

Dickie Smith, the indefatigable comrade of my Moffat days, has sailed for the Middle East - ⅔ of his course went with him - the rest were posted home. It was pretty crusty cheese that I wasn't among the more favoured ones, although the ME is alright, don't you know, and a damned sight better than India or the Far East. In fact, if I go there, I shan't worry too much, although you cannot realise just how grand it would be to see my people and my darling again and especially to tell her just how much I love her because that is something she hasn't heard me say yet.

Oh Ivy, you're going to see an awful change in me, I know. For one thing, my moustache is bigger and all wild. I am bigger myself in every dimension because I have lived on all the butter in the world for a year and a half.

And, more important, I have seen so much more of every kind of people, so much more of life and a little of death - and the whole has been a profounder and sadder experience than I knew before. But I don't worry - and don't you - for if I have lost any youth, I shall recapture it with you and we shall relive the former happiness. Oh, I know that the dream world I have lived amongst since I left England and all that I loved, is soon going to crystallise into reality. Only for a little longer will this dreaming be, and then, and then ... Until then, my love, it is all yours, whose other could it ever be,

Lovingly, Philip.

*Philip Spencer's grave and the
East Bank Cemetery in East
London, Cape Province, South
Africa. An inscription on the
stone quotes his beloved Shelley:
"He has outsoared the shadow
of our night."*

Chapter Four

Finding a New Future

Work was my saviour in my grief, despite the looming bulk of Pendle Hill nearby. In that blankness I had to sort myself out. Thank goodness, I still had chalk in my hair and my teaching kept me going. I kept in touch with Philip's family but we were all suffering the same sorrow.

I spent two years at Higham Village School. My predecessor had been perfect, apparently, and I was always hearing, "Miss Lawson did this and Miss Lawson did that" but I just thought, "Miss Starkie's going to do her bit."

Christmas was coming and the children were excited, which helped to take my mind off things. Few people ever mentioned Philip to me as they hadn't known him or that we had become engaged the day he set sail. I don't know how much he had told his mother. At that time, anyone much over 40 had been born a Victorian and the stultifying attitudes of that era still stifled natural openness, especially among the middle and upper classes.

Teaching kept me busy and I was grateful for that. I had 20 in my class aged from five to eight, which was hard work, for it was a typical village school with two teachers plus the head. At that time no child had the right to a proper secondary education. A select few like myself got grammar school scholarships but otherwise it meant paying fees and things changed only in the late 1940s.

Most children attended one school for all their educational years until 14, so some were bigger than me. If ever the headmistress went out, I'd be ordered in to play the piano and practise hymns with these huge lads clanking around in their clogs - wooden-soled leather boots - and I was terrified. Of course they tried it on a bit with a young teacher but I soon got the measure of them.

Many of the parents worked in the cotton industry or in farming. Adding to our workload were evacuees, in our case from Mousehole in Cornwall. Can you imagine it? They were talking Cornish and we were talking Lancashire, the accents mixing and rising to the rafters.

The parents were often more bother than the children. I was artistic and at Easter helped the children to make cards. One father turned up drunk from the quaintly-named Four Alls pub nearby. He came bustling in, carrying his children's cards. "I'm not having you giving my children this rubbish to bring home," he said, and with that he tore them up.

I was scared but told him that all children would do Easter cards and he drifted away, muttering. In sailed Mrs Stephenson, the head, and seeing me upset gave me this advice, which has stood me in good stead since.

"The first thing you say is that you will sue him for libel, then tell him he's trespassing on Lancashire County Council premises. If you come out with big words like that, it scares them off."

Pendle Hill had become an Army training ground and we lectured the children on the dangers of picking up anything they found discarded, for the slopes were covered with ammunition, some spent and some still dangerous. One boy was messing about in class and it was obvious he had something in his pocket. Following the advice given at my teacher training college, I told him to come to the front and put whatever it was in the basket on my desk. He sauntered grumpily towards me and threw down his precious object. It clunked into the basket and I found myself looking at part of a mortar bomb, still packed with explosive. It's a wonder I'm still here to tell the tale. I gave it to the caretaker, who got rid of it.

We had to take the children to church services occasionally and I'd be left in charge of them while Mrs Stephenson played the organ. I'd get the children settled nicely into their pews, which were towards the back, then join in the singing, the curate's tenor voice booming beside me. Then I'd look up from my hymn book and see all the little ones at the front - they'd crawled under the pews.

At home we had two evacuee children billeted on us from the slums of Manchester. One was very dirty and badly clothed. My mother was typical Lancashire and had to scrub everything twice, so it was hard for her to cope with this invasion of her neat and clean home. I suppose those evacuees might still be around, so I'll call them Doris and Colin, who were both 11. They weren't related.

Mother used to strip Doris down, give her a thorough wash and put her in some of my old clothes which I had long grown out of. Every now and again, when there was a lull in the bombing of Manchester, Mother would give the two evacuees half a crown each to go home on the bus to visit their families.

Dressed smartly when she left, Doris would turn up on the Sunday night in dirty old rags. My mother asked, "Where are your lovely clothes?" to which Doris would reply, in a very matter of fact way, "Mum's flogged them." We'd ask her how she'd spent the weekend and she'd say, "We went knocking off in Woolworths!" A bigger girl would knock goods off their stands for Doris to catch and steal.

I was appalled! What a terrible start in life. How could we teach her anything when this was normal for her. I hope maybe she went back home a slightly better person at the end of her stay with us , for I used to have long talks with her. They weren't with us for long, less than a year.

It was the other extreme with Colin, who went to a smart but very strict Catholic school and went round telling us that we Methodists were no good. We could never leave Doris alone or she would have gone through the house and everything would have been taken back to Manchester. So, although she was a Catholic, we had to take her with us to chapel and were criticized by the local Catholic priest for doing so. My father gave him a very curt answer to that.

It was something of a relief to me to be at school where I felt I had more control over the behaviour of my pupils. It wasn't always easy for them to concentrate. Some children had done several hours' work on the farm before coming to school and, once inside the warm classroom, fell asleep on their desks, heads cradled in their arms.

Not long after I arrived, one of His Majesty's Inspectors of Schools arrived, unannounced as always. My headmistress came into my classroom pretending to borrow a chair. I knew full well she had enough chairs in her room and she mouthed, "HMI!" at me.

When he came in, we were singing a song about Nature's wonders and he said with disapproval, "You're teaching these children to worship Nature!" to which I replied, "Yes, just look through that window, that's Nature all round us, the beauty of it. Perhaps it's different in the towns!"

After two years at Higham, in 1944, I moved to another primary school at Barrow, which was much closer to home and avoided a tortuous journey. My headmistress was leaving and it seemed a good moment to move on. The new school was very close to the Army barracks. The infants would run in excitedly and tell me, "So-and-so has got a balloon!" and it was a contraceptive. The soldiers seemed to find our playground wall a convenient and sheltered place conducive to romance, shall we call it.

I wasn't married then, just an innocent young teacher, but I knew what this 'balloon' really was and told them to put it in the waste bin. Teacher training college had taught me nothing about how to deal with mortar bombs and used contraceptives in the classroom. I had to grow up very fast.

In 1945 the war ended but I felt an outsider to all the street parties and processions. I put on the brave face which was my constant companion in the outside world. I had shut myself off from social life and put my soul into my teaching. Eventually, my friends told me, "Come on Ivy, you can't stay at home all the time. You're coming out with us. There are soldiers in Barrow and Poles based in Clitheroe."

Reluctantly, I started going out and about and one day in 1947, on the bus to a concert in Blackburn, I met John, who was to become my husband. The bus had come from Clitheroe where he was based and I was getting on with my friend Terry at Whalley. So packed was the bus that we were hanging on precariously, swaying on the open platform, the road rushing past below us, for there were no doors then.

Two good looking Polish army officers were also jammed

47

into the crowd but, gallantly, they managed to find two seats for my friend and I, so we squeezed on to one of the two long bench-type seats which faced each other over the wheel arch.

Andreas was the more talkative one and obviously after girls. He was married, as it turned out, but we were immediately on our guard anyway. Terry said quietly in my ear, "I don't him but I like the other one."

Andreas leaned over to chat to us and asked us where we were going. John, who was 'the other one', was much quieter but when I said we were off to a concert, he looked interested. He was a great music lover.

I later learned that he spoke four languages, Polish, German, Italian and Russian, and was now picking up English quickly. In his accented voice, he asked slowly, "Where are you going?" I had my score of The Messiah and told him we were headed for King George's Hall, Blackburn, to hear it. He and Andreas were heading for Tony's, a low dive in Blackburn, but John said he would prefer to come to the concert with us instead.

I was alarmed. "I can't go to the concert with a Polish officer!" I thought to myself. It was assumed, at the time, that girls who went around with soldiers they hardly knew were rather 'fast'.

Isobel Baillie was the soprano and Kathleen Ferrier, whose hometown was Blackburn, was the contralto. John sat next to me and shared my score to follow the words and music. I thought, "He must be alright if he'll go to something religious like this." When I asked him his name, he said, "Jan" but of course it was the Polish pronunciation of "Yan" and I said, "Oh, that's John" and so it was from then on. As we parted afterwards, he said, "I will see you again. If

Lieutenant Jan Wojszcz, whom everyone came to know as John

I come next week, will you be there?" Instead, I invited him to come for supper. Families living near military camps, as we did, often invited small groups of soldiers into their homes, knowing they would be missing their own homes and families.

So the following week, this handsome, blue-eyed Polish officer arrived and my parents gave him a warm welcome. We were all musical and played the piano together and sang.

A keen photographer, even under the most trying circumstances, John brought pictures he had taken during his tumultuous war years and showed them to us all, picking up a few new English words as he went. When we first met he had only a few English phrases but already I could see his quick mind lapping up new vocabulary. We were all impressed by his gallantry and the clicking of his heels.

John was an extremely clever and resourceful person and later bound his photos into a lovely book with a linen cover. Fabric was in short supply, so I asked him, "Where did you get that linen?" and he replied, "That's my coffin." All soldiers had been issued with a linen bodybag.

Life had been very busy for me, with a full time job and volunteer work running a YMCA centre for service people. My sister Alice and I had set up the centre in Whalley some years before to give those from the nearby military camps somewhere to go for a snack and a chat and pick up some cigarettes. Centres like ours sprang up all over the country.

We also set up a magazine called Contact to send to all lads from our area who were serving away from home. That was a huge effort, using a typewriter and carbon copies.

Alice and I always seemed to end up with the worst shift at the centre, Friday night, a very busy time, but Alice was home only at weekends from her job in Manchester. It was a big commitment for us but we felt we had to do our bit. Most of them were grand lads. Alice and I would play the piano for them and sing songs, calling ourselves Pandemonium and Nostalgia.

We got friendly with the Devon Regiment who were stationed nearby and one day they said, "We must do something for you in return" and came up with a full regimental band. I'd already sung with that band in the Assembly Rooms and whenever I turned up for a dance, they played 'my song', a 1943 hit called Mairzy Doats including a line, "and little lambs eat ivy".

We put up posters but didn't know what we were in for. They brought the whole band to play in the little Methodist Church Sunday School and the place lit up. The minister, who had hardly ever lifted a finger to help any of these lads stationed near us, nor the local ones who had been sent away, turned up to find out what all the noise was about. "Who's in charge here?" he demanded. My sister, older than I and with a lot more clout, said, "I am, actually, but it should be you. We're doing this to raise money for the Contact magazine for local lads who are serving away."

He was furious. "You're not licensed for dancing!" he cried.

"We're not dancing," said my sister. Actually, we were on and off but it was just a nice musical evening with supper. It was a wonderful night. There were other regiments which came and went but we were very fond of the Devons. They taught us to talk Devon and we taught them Lancashire.

Catering for the military meant we could get food for the canteen that was rarely seen at home, including huge tins of processed meat called Spam which Alice and I struggled to open, handing them over to our customers to prise apart for us. There was Camp concentrated coffee in bottles and tins of Horlicks, not very exciting but a hot drink was what they wanted after a cold day training on Pendle.

They'd come in soaked and weary and order, "Twenty cups of tea and you," to which I'd reply that I was not on the menu. There was a lot of banter but most of them were just trying to forget the real battles that were ahead of them. Many were headed for the invasion of France in 1944 and some didn't come home again.

I had qualified for St. John Ambulance and Red Cross nursing. My sister and I would visit wounded or sick military personnel at the local hospital on Sunday afternoons where patients well enough to be up wore blue suits and white shirts. That was hard work because, once they were feeling better, they could be a bit wild and do silly things like find a bicycle and ride up and down the ward.

After the D-Day invasion of 1944, wounded soldiers were ferried back to hospitals all over England and as soon as the first arrived locally, I went straight up to see how I could help. It was a grim sight. Surgeons were operating day and night amputating limbs and trying to put these young men back together again. To see these lads trying to come to terms with terrible, life-changing injuries was harrowing.

I got a medal for services to the community for all my work, though I wouldn't dream of wearing it and when John saw it in the box, he roared with laughter and called it my Spam medal. I said firmly, "I earned that!"

Chapter Five

John's Journey

When I met John, a few years after the war, he was a Captain in the Royal Engineers in the British Army. His life had been completely overturned by conflict. He was born Jan Wojszcz in Blonie near Warsaw in 1915. His father was away at the war and when he returned, little Jan didn't realise who it was.

In 1939, he had not long completed his degree in civil engineering at Warsaw University when Poland was attacked by both Germany and Russia. In England, we learned a terrifying new word, Blitzkrieg, meaning lightning war, in which Poland had been left shattered after a few weeks of crushing attacks.

The German Luftwaffe knocked out the railway system and shot the Polish air force out of the sky. Half the country was absorbed into the Nazi Third Reich, the other into Communist Russia. Officially, Poland had ceased to exist but remained strong in the hearts of the Polish people.

An estimated 60,000 Poles were killed, 200,000 were wounded and 700,000 were taken prisoner. John's brother was taken to the notorious Dachau concentration camp where he died. John himself, who had been in a cadet group at university, was ordered to fight on the side of the

German Army. Later, when Germany tore up its pact with Russia and attacked her, John was captured by the Russians. He was herded with thousands of others, both men and women, into cattle trucks. As the doors were barred shut on the crush of bodies, he had no idea where he would end up or if he would survive.

Sanitary conditions were appalling and, as the hours passed and the train rumbled along slowly, those in the truck had to bury their pride and use a corner of the floor as a toilet. The deprivation endured was terrible, he told me, and it breaks my heart to think of him as a young man, snatched up from his life and treated with such cruelty.

Their destination was a concentration camp in Siberia to which they were marched after being dumped at the side of the railway track. On arrival there was little to greet them and they were forced to build their own huts in terrible weather. Seeing others dying around him, John determined, "They're not going to get the better of me!"

Inmates were half starved and given little protection from the intense cold. Once shoes wore out, there were no replacements and John told me they tied rags round their feet.

Because he was good at languages, John began to pick up Russian. The peasants who lived around the camp had some sympathy with the prisoners for Stalin's rule was often as harsh towards his own people as to his 'enemies'. Through the bitterness of the Siberian winter, they would creep up to the camp boundary and push raw onions through the wire fencing to the inmates. That was all they could spare from their own sparse stores.

Anything with flavour was a treat compared to their bland and monotonous diet and John developed such a taste for onions that when he came to England, he ate a great many of them, much to my surprise.

When I teased him about it, he pointed out that being deprived of sweet things had been very good for his teeth. "I have all my own teeth, you haven't all yours!" he would retaliate and he was right.

Life in the camp was very hard but prisoners found small ways to cling to hope. Bones found in soup could be moulded to make a crucifix and people prayed for someone, something, to come to their rescue. They had very little news of the outside world and no idea how long they would be prisoners.

John's flair for languages almost cost him his life. He began to understand what was being said around him in Russian and translated for the other prisoners. Suddenly he was labeled a spy, marched out and subjected to water torture, laid down with a constant drip, drip, drip on the forehead.

"You don't feel the first few," he told me, "but by the time you have had it on for an hour, it's like a hammer."

When not being tortured, John was kept in a narrow wooden cell with room neither to sit nor stand upright.

In a further act of sadism, he and other suspects were led out, ordered to dig their own graves and stand beside the hole to be shot. John saw the guards line up with their guns, heard the shots and fell, the pure shock of the moment causing him to believe he had been killed. He had not. All the bullets were dummies.

"We all fell," he recalled. "We all thought we were dead." The aim had been to make the prisoners confess but most had nothing to admit and were not spies. Then they were taken back to their camps and locked in cells. The stick having failed to yield any secrets, the Russians tried a carrot. They put a pretty young Russian girl into his cell to see if she could get any information out of him. That didn't work either.

Feeling he had little to lose, John decided to escape and, despite being recaptured several times with the constant threat of being shot dead, continued to do so until at last, he got away completely. I don't know exactly what happened at this point but somehow John joined up with the Polish General, Wladyslaw Anders.

In June 1941, after Germany ripped up its treaty with Russia and turned on her former ally, Russia sought an alliance with Britain. Part of this new agreement was the setting up of a Polish fighting unit, called the Polish II Corps. Many prisoners of the Russians were now handed over to serve in this Army.

At the end of 1942, the 'Anders Army' troops left the Soviet Union, joining the British High Command in the Middle East, travelling through Iran, Iraq and Palestine.

In some ways it was out of the frying pan and into the fire for John, who fought in some of the most decisive and deadly battles of World War II. The Polish II Corps went to Africa, fighting alongside the British 8ᵗʰ Army in the bloodbath of the Western Desert and, once the Germans had been defeated there, moved across the Mediterranean Sea and up into Italy.

Here, 3,500 Poles were among those who lost their lives taking part in the final capture of Monte Cassino in May 1944, a German stronghold. Following a four-month siege, this historic hilltop monastery was reduced to a ruin.

In an act of outstanding bravery, John was badly injured and was later awarded the Military Cross. It was only many

Above: John (left) in Russia, 1942, with fellow Polish officers
Right: John in Siberia after escaping from the prison camp

years later that I discovered he had this medal, given only to those who have acted way beyond the call of duty. He didn't mention it to me. Only when I was doing his ribbons for a reunion did I see something unusual. "What's this for?" I asked.

He told me that after five days of bombardment, his sergeant came to him and said a mine had been dropped but failed to explode. Now it had to be defused. "It's a new one to me," the sergeant told him, "I don't know how it operates." John sent all his men back to the trench and did the job himself, knowing that at any moment he could be blown to pieces. But he was not willing to leave it there to kill others. I asked him, "Did you have to do that?" and he replied, "I was the officer, I was in charge, I had to do it."

Carefully, John removed the battery and the mine began to hiss. He hurled it away but caught the full blast. His men thought he'd been killed and left him for dead but his batman waited and dragged him out of the line of bombardment. Badly injured, he was given wine, which was the wrong thing to do for someone bleeding badly but it was Italy and they had little else.

Soon he was whisked away from the battle to a military hospital, his head and hands swathed in bandages. Like many people involved in horrific events, John used humour to get over it. He liked to tease me by describing how, with bandaged hands, he was unable to use the toilet alone and kept calling for his batman to help. Of course there was no batman, only a nurse for whom such aid was just part of the job. I said, "That's your story!"

After recovering, John returned to active service. The end of the war brought little respite for him as, working with the Royal Engineers, he took part in the endless job

Above: John receiving the Military Cross for outstanding bravery in dealing with an unexploded mine which had resulted in severe injuries to his hands (right)

*The memorial at Monte Cassino to the many Poles who
died there and which John helped to construct*

*Left: Part of
the ruins of
the monastery*

of clearing mines and unexploded bombs from battlefields. He also helped to build a memorial on Monte Cassino to the Poles who lost their lives there. The inscription reads: "For your freedom and ours, we gave our lives to the world, our hearts to Poland and our souls to God".

Not only was his work on the battlefields not finished but John felt he had nowhere else to go. Most Polish people were embittered that Britain and America had failed to ensure Poland's independence and had allowed the Russians to stay.

In the end he and many other Poles, who found themselves among millions of displaced people in Europe, came to England. He arrived in Clitheroe as a Captain in the Royal Engineers and was sent to what was then Low Moor Mill. As soon as he saw the Ribble Valley, he fell in love with it, revelling in its lush greenness after the harsh, dry landscapes of the African desert and Southern Europe.

John and I struck up a deep friendship, fostered by our shared love of music and the countryside and our work together in teaching English to other Polish soldiers. Gradually, I picked up some of the Polish language.

After his first visit to my home, John came to see us whenever he was free and became like one of the family. At that point, I had no idea of any more serious involvement and had been frank from the beginning that I was still grieving for Philip. When he asked to see me more often, I said, "I'm not really ready to be with anybody."

He was also honest with me, telling me about Mary, his Polish nurse who had cared for him after his injuries at Monte Cassino. She had persuaded him to resist the doctor's recommendation of amputation and he was very grateful to her. "If they take my hands, they take my life," he had told her. Mary spent hour after hour with him, cleaning his wounds and taking out the shrapnel. One small piece remained in his thumb for the rest of his life and he'd jiggle it around sometimes but otherwise his hands healed well.

When we heard that Mary would be in Andover, Hampshire, for Christmas, I encouraged John to go to see her. I spent the time wondering how much of a girlfriend she was to him. On his return, he told me, "Whenever we went for a walk, we'd stop by a wall, and what was growing over it? Ivy! So I knew I had to come back to you." I had always hated my name but for once it had come in useful.

My parents liked him until he wanted to marry me. Not only was he a foreigner but he was also of a different religion, being a Lutheran. In those days, there was a great deal of prejudice against marriages between people of different nationalities and faiths. A friend of the family said, "He's bound to be alright. Look at his blue eyes!" for people associated blue eyes with Western European characteristics, rather than those of the East. Silly, really.

There was no dramatic proposal of marriage, for he was 33 by this time and I was 27. I was in Bradford Infirmary after having appendicitis and John came to see me. "Let's get married, then I can look after you," he said. I thought how lovely that would be and agreed, very happily. He knew me well, saying, "We've both lost everything". Now it was time to build a new life together.

Our feelings at that moment are best summed up in the words of Richard Hillary, an RAF pilot, in his book The Last Enemy. Hillary, an RAF pilot, was disfigured in a crash but returned to flying, only to meet his last enemy - death - in 1943. He wrote, "True happiness is never a stagnant thing, it is a case of destroying a sanctuary to build a sanctuary."

I felt that was true for John and I, we had to build again. Mother came to visit me in hospital the evening after our engagement had been arranged and John arrived with a beautiful bevelled mirror for me, on which he had written, "Will you marry me?"

My mother was taken aback for she and my father were still in the Victorian age but I stood up to them this time. I regretted that Philip and I had not married quickly on a special licence. We could have snatched a little time together. I wasn't going to miss out on the chance of a happy married life with John and had all kinds of battles over it. My father even threatened not to bring me to church.

People in Whalley, often unaware of how much those like John had sacrificed and how great their contribution had been to winning the war, would say to my mother, "Those Poles are all over the place getting drunk! He'll go back to Poland and leave her with twins." They wouldn't dare say it to me.

My parents' opposition to my marriage was stupid because they liked John. My father would play chess with him and my mother would be singing with him at the piano. In the end they had to come round for we weren't going to change our minds. In later life, my parents came to rely on John to help them in the garden and with repairs to their home.

We were married on July 10th 1948 at Whalley Methodist Church. When I called round to see the Minister and make the arrangements, I said, "Reverend, will you marry me?" and he replied, "I would, but I've a wife inside."

John and I had several meetings with the Minister before the wedding at which John expressed his worries, not about being a good husband to me but about what other people were saying. The Minister told us to take no notice. For all their bluster, my parents were both at the wedding. Our reception was a simple but very happy affair at the Swan Hotel in our village. Although the war was over, this was a period of austerity for Britain as we paid back enormous debts run up to manufacture armaments and supply the Forces.

Many homes had been destroyed or needed extensive repairs. Most luxury goods were exported to make money for the country and were hard to get in Britain. Some foods were still rationed because so much was needed to feed the millions of hungry people in Europe, where farming and industry had been devastated.

To buy clothes, you needed ration coupons so, like many brides at that time, I didn't wear a long dress but a very smart two-piece suit in ice blue and a straw hat trimmed with little blue flowers. Our wedding was no less happy for a lack of frills.

My sister Alice had been married not long before and she had worn a bridal gown but I didn't have the coupons and didn't think it was important. John certainly didn't think it was important.

A taxi took John and his best man from their barracks to the church and the same driver then collected my father and I, saying, "It's alright, they're waiting for you and they're stone, cold sober!" That was the reputation Poles had and I knew they could drink but John wasn't like that.

The church was packed for there was a certain morbid curiosity in the village to see if I really would go ahead and marry this Pole. He had learned the marriage service by heart to prove to all that he could speak English.

Some of John's Polish friends were at the service. Those

The wedding of Ivy and John, 1948

who were Catholics had been warned by a Catholic Englishwoman that if they attended our wedding in the Methodist Church, they would no longer be welcome at Mass.

My parents had stopped short of inviting John's Polish friends to the wedding reception but when we arrived at the hotel, they were waiting in the bar. John and I joined them for a drink as our guests made their way upstairs to our reception. Philip's parents were there and I suggested they also went up but Mrs Spencer said they wouldn't be able to sit down until the bride was there. She was very prim and proper and I thought, "I've done it wrong again!" However, they were very happy for me that I had managed to find a good man in John.

As the time for speeches came, I astonished everyone by announcing that I would make a speech, unheard of for the bride then, and played some Polish songs on the piano. At that point I was Ivy Wojszcz but later we decided to be Mr and Mrs Starkie, partly because so many people had problems pronouncing John's name, let alone spelling it.

Our honeymoon was spent at the Waterhead Hotel on the lake in Ambleside. John was thrilled. "This is like the Polish lakes, Zakopane," he said. "I'm back home." After that we tried to return each Whitsun when the Lakes are at their most beautiful.

When invited to John's dances at the Officers' Mess,
we'd have a few tame English dances, waltzes etc,
then the whole place would erupt with Polish
dances, the polka, mazurka etc. The Polish girls
wore such beautiful costumes. I felt, at last, that
the bleak years after Philip's death had lifted and,
yes, "We are the music- makers, we are the dream-
ers of dreams". How could I not love this man?

Chapter Six

The House That John Built

It was usual for women to leave their professions on marriage and so I left my post at Barrow but was soon approached by the chairman of the managers of Read Congregational School between Padiham and Whalley, begging me to take on the headship there temporarily because he had heard of my good reputation.

I wasn't keen for I wanted to be free to enjoy married life but was persuaded to accept and so in September, went back to work.

Nobody would acknowledge John's skills as a civil engineer because he was Polish but this made him more determined to prove them all wrong. For the time being, after leaving the Army, he had to be content with a job at Accrington Brick and Tile Works which he got because his father had had a brickworks in Warsaw and John could work a gas kiln.

I worried about him in the muck of the brickworks doing a job beneath his ability but he'd just look at his hands and say, "If I've got these, I can show them I can work." Now, having learned English, he had to learn 'Lancashire'. He'd come home asking me what phrases like 'up yonder' meant. Our first home was wonderful. We bought a plot of land in Whalley and built a new house, in the meantime living with my parents, which didn't really work out, but then it rarely does, does it? My mother thought that because she had always spent every hour cleaning and scrubbing, I should too, but I wanted to be out with John.

My savings paid for the plot of land and John said, "I'll get the bricks, I'll build the house." Of course we were both working all day and we had to have a builder but also did a lot ourselves. I got a bit fed up, saying, "Let's go the pictures" and John would say, "That costs half a crown (12½p). I can get three bricks for that."

But it was an exciting time. We went all the way into Manchester to choose our bathroom suite. When complete, it was a lovely house, three bedroom detached, and we were so thrilled to have it. It was the house that John built and is still there. We named it Witch Elms, after the witches of Pendle, and had a wych elm tree in the garden. John made a weather vane in the shape of a witch.

Our new garden was bare and John worked late in the evening to turn it into something special. A street light stood just outside and neighbours teased me that he worked until midnight by its glow. He was very proud of his home. It meant more to him than most to have somewhere to call his own.

We were both very happy to discover that we were to have a child and Tim was born in 1949. I gave up my job and there followed our happiest years, despite being desperately short of money.

John and I had made a pact between us that we would have a child as soon as possible and not wait until we were better off. I'm so glad we did, for there we were in the house that John built in a lovely area of Whalley with a little baby.

Witch Elms, the house that John built in 1950

With Tim as a baby

It was lovely. John's experiences in the war had made him into a man who always tried to do what was right, even if it flouted convention. Throughout my labour, he stayed by my side and saw Tim born which was almost unheard of then. The midwife couldn't believe it. He helped me to breathe the gas and air provided for pain relief and when the canister threatened to run out, he demanded another instantly.

In the midst of all this, I remember asking, "How's my mother?" to which John replied, "Don't worry about your mother, she's having the hysterics for you."

Having a child meant even more to John than it did to most fathers, for here was his own flesh and blood. His brother Romek had died in the concentration camp and he never saw his parents again. They and his sister Mary survived the war but were told John had been killed in the blast at Monte Cassino, only discovering he was alive when he wrote to them himself.

John's mother was diabetic and we sent drugs and other things which she couldn't get behind the Iron Curtain. Friends wrote letters in carefully coded language warning John not to return as he would be labelled an enemy of the Communist state. Others who had gone back had disappeared, including Andreas.

It meant a great deal to John when eventually, as restrictions eased a little, his niece Joanne was able to visit us but he never lost the feeling that one day he could be arrested again.

Pushing Tim in his shining Silver Cross pram was a joy to both of us, crossing the road and going up the lane towards Pendle. Once he could talk, Tim had a favourite tree, a big old one, and always insisted we walk up to what he called the "woeful tree" after a story we read together, an old tree stump looking rather sinister. Tim talked before he walked and would say, "The woeful tree looks awful," which made us laugh. By the time we got back he'd usually be sound asleep and I'd wheel him into the lounge, leaving him in his commodious transport for a nap.

So that I could get on with things, I put him in a playpen, much to his indignation, thinking that, no matter how much he complained, he couldn't escape. Nor could he, but found instead that the pen could be shuffled along towards the door, so that was one up to him.

By now, John's employers had recognised some of his true talents and moved him into the drawing office at the brickworks. As soon as he came home from work, he'd play with Tim. Walking in through the door from the bus stop, John would put out his arms and cry, "Hello my darling!" then walk straight past me to scoop up Tim. That was alright, for I knew how much I meant to him.

Later, when Tim was still quite young, I worked as a supply teacher and my parents looked after him. When he was five and went to school, I went back to work full time, back to chalk in my hair again.

Throughout this time, John was haunted by a fear that, having lost everything once, it could happen again. For four years, he fought for British citizenship until at last, in 1952, it was granted. This meant a great deal to him. Deep inside, John had never lost his fear that somehow he would one day be forced to return to Poland, now under Russian control.

This was no irrational fear. White Russians who opposed the Communist regime had already been sent by the Allies to face execution in the Soviet Union in one of many tragic political games played after the so-called peace of 1945. My uncle, who was a solicitor, offered to guide us through this legal minefield for no fee if we would take on the name Starkie, for this was my old family surname. And so it was that John became a British citizen and we were Mr and Mrs Starkie.

I would have been quite happy to remain a Wojszcz but in a way I think John was keen to leave that name behind. He never said it but I think he always had a deep-rooted fear of being traced by the Communists who now considered him an enemy. He had escaped so many times from his prison camp that he had ended up with a sentence of 13 years and feared that somehow he could be reclaimed and sent to Siberia to complete his term. It might seem a bizarre fear now, but terrible things happened in Eastern Europe after the war and I can quite understand his worries. It is a common fear of those who have lost everything that it could happen again.

Neither did he want our son Tim, who had been christened Wojszcz, to be singled out as different. John had to put up with English people assuming that foreigners were deaf. My father would shout loudly at him, "How do you like England?" adding, as if he wasn't there, "He's from Poland, you know."

"His name's John! Call him John," I'd protest. Fortunately, a sense of humour remained indomitable within John and he was able to appreciate the farce of it all where others might have taken offence. He was always courteous, a perfect gentleman, and was respected wherever he went, making friends easily.

Yet he boiled inside when faced by more deep-seated foolishness or self-centred behaviour, for years of deprivation had left him with clear views of what was important and what was not. Everything was black and white with no grey areas. Years later, in the middle of a silly row, I said I was leaving and he said, "I'll pack your bag for you!" and that shut me up.

I became so used to his accent that I stopped noticing it but every now and again, when he was tired, John would put things back to front where two nouns had been joined together, such as mat door instead of doormat, or step door.

So strongly did he feel about speaking the language of his adopted country that he felt it was wrong at Polish Army reunions to lapse into Polish, even with his former countrymen. I spoke a little Polish but couldn't write it, though I learned that "sz" is "sh" and "cz" is "ch". He never wanted to take an active part in the Polish community, which was quite strong.

Gradually he was accepted as one of the English community, going to chapel and eventually becoming a Freemason. I remember him walking our lovely chow dog down by the river, after we had moved, rehearsing his words for the ceremony.

When Tim started school, I wanted to work full time but couldn't get a job at the village school because I wasn't Church of England, though I had been good enough to do supply for them. Parents petitioned the vicar in my favour, but he was not to be moved.

In 1954 we uprooted from our beloved home and headed across the border to Yorkshire to make a new life in Grassington. John had got nowhere with applications to Lancashire County Council who refused to take him on as a civil engineer. I felt sorry for him because he deserved better than being in the brickworks. It wasn't a bad job but he was capable of more. West Riding County Council, as it was then, had more vision and he became a surveyor with them. He kept saying, "I'll show them" and he did.

Whenever I drive along the M62, crossing the boundary from Yorkshire to Lancashire, I think of John. There's a bridge called The Rainbow Bridge on which he was the chief engineer when the motorway was being built. It was so cold in winter that on one occasion he had to take the young lad working with him to the pub for a brandy to thaw him out. To John, it was a hardship but nothing like what he had experienced in Russia.

I now applied for the headship of Threshfield Primary School, scouting out the area first and even knocking on the door of the assistant teacher who, it turned out, had also applied for the job. I felt a bit awful about that but it was the world of work. Into Manchester I went and bought a Hebe sports suit, with a box-pleated skirt and jacket. Hebe was an extremely smart designer label now much in demand among vintage clothes fans. It certainly boosted my self confidence, which was just as well, for the managers fired some fierce questions at me. "Do you lose your temper?" demanded one. I felt like saying I could if provoked but restrained myself.

I knew that headmasters were usually offered a council house but was told that obviously I, as a woman, would not. Loftily, I replied, "I have a brand new house to sell."

They must have liked the fact that I stood up for myself for soon I found myself in charge of a very unusual little school.

Chapter Seven

A Country Headmistress

Threshfield School sits among fields with no other building in sight, its stern, gritstone apparently looking for a better audience than the many rabbits bouncing around nearby. Well might it stand on its dignity, for Threshfield, a grand old lady of the educational world, has been improving the minds of young people since 1674.

Its remote location is accounted for by the poor quality of the land on which it stands, a thin layer of soil over hard limestone, which was donated by benefactors as being the least missed by the sheep. The earliest masters taught Latin and Greek with the aim of getting the boys, for it was only boys then, into Cambridge or Oxford universities.

The main building has mullioned windows and a large stone porch above which is a small room, once home to the headmaster. There was also an assistant, called an usher. Our main door was heavy, studded wood opened by an enormous iron key.

Home for John, Tim and I was a house we bought in Grassington village nearby and later we moved to another property in the same village with a gorgeous view down to the river and across to my school on the other side where

Threshfield School

Tim joined me as a pupil. The first time I saw Threshfield School, I was thrilled by its sense of history. But it was a bleak place in 1954, with no drainage or running water and only chemical toilets, and I complained about such primitive conditions at every meeting of the school managers until something was done. I felt it was an insult to the children to offer such a raw deal.

When, after years of protest, the toilets were replaced, my local education officer at Skipton, whom I had harangued long and hard about the problem, telephoned and said, "Now you've got your nice new toilets, put a ribbon across. I'm coming to open them!" And he did.

All did not run smoothly. One day a small girl returned from the new toilets soaking wet. "I pulled the chain and the whole thing came down on me!" she wailed. Rushing to inspect the damage, I was faced by a Niagara Falls of water from a whole line of cisterns which, because of the intense condensation in our cold outbuilding, had slid from their brackets. In those days, they were hung high on the wall and operated by a chain which hung down. Something had gone badly wrong, my small girl hadn't the strength to cause such a disaster even if she'd wanted to.

It is at moments like these that a village school headmistress must gather all her resources. She must be an electrician, a plumber - the lot. There was no phone and nobody close by to help so we fixed it ourselves, with some of the bigger lads helping me to restore the cisterns to their brackets. They loved it, of course, especially the getting wet part.

At one time, after the only other teacher left, I was the only adult in the school and had no phone. It was years before one arrived, installed in the stock room which became my office. I looked in some frustration at the new local secondary school which seemed to get whatever it wanted, some of it unnecessary in my view, when I was fighting for basic services.

Staffing levels fluctuated but usually I had one other teacher. At this time, she lived just along the road and did not even have running water at her cottage. At break time some of the boys would fill a milk churn from our new tap and carry it home for her. She did, however, have a phone and allowed me to use it.

During the often bitter winters of Upper Wharfedale, we were always cold. Storage radiators were a recent addition, warm in the morning but cool by the afternoon, and we were grateful for the two iron stoves, one at each end of the room, which we kept fed with coke. In winter, the fireguards encircling them became festooned with wet gloves and coats. Snow did not close schools then as now for children were used to walking and staff tended to be nearby. If the roads were closed, some of the children had a wonderful romp across the tops to reach Threshfield where lessons would begin only after our home-made snow plough of a plank on a rope had cleared a path across the playground and, vitally, to the toilets. This was normal winter life for them.

At first, there were only 35 pupils and one teacher besides me. I walked on eggshells for a while for I knew that my sole adult companion had wanted my job but we ended up by getting on very well. The pupil/teacher ratio offered a similar one-to-one attention as in a private school, which you can't beat at primary level.

All my pupils could read before they were six and then they were away. The school's reputation increased to the point at which I had a waiting list of those wanting to join. Psychology plays a vital part in teaching. I knew I had to learn how to communicate with my young charges.

At first they were wild, having been without a head teacher for a while, running around all over the place. Yet when I told them to sit still they did so and never moved. Neither state was right and I worked to foster a mutual understanding and respect which fell somewhere between their natural exuberance and my need for discipline. To achieve this, it was necessary for me to get inside their heads and see things from their point of view.

"I'm going to say good morning to you every day when I come to school and I hope you'll say it back to me," I advised them early on. Their little faces looked slightly quizzical but after that, as I came through the gate and strode across our big playground, we did say our good mornings. All except one, a lad of 11 who was bigger than I. His silence puzzled me, for it lacked the sharp edge of downright defiance. It was John who came up with the solution. With his keen ear for language and his long study of human nature, he noted that local people didn't tend to say good morning but often greeted each other with a broad Yorkshire, "Na then!" If they passed each other in their Land Rovers, this greeting would be reduced to the raising of a single finger while the others remained fixed firmly to the steering wheel.

The next morning I walked across the playground, saying good morning, but as I reached this lad I said, "Na then, Leslie!" His eyes darted up swiftly to meet mine and he replied, "Na then, Mrs Starkie!" I was in, it was open sesame and from then on he was quick to do any heavy job I might need help with.

Later, when I became involved with a women's professional group, I would emphasise the importance of communication. It's not enough to write rules and regulations, you have got to get down to the inner man.

They gave me stick for being from Lancashire. "We always beat you at cricket!" they'd say. "Not always," I replied, standing my corner, "the red rose will come to the top." I had to learn a new language. They all said, "I aren't" as in "I aren't going there!" I'd tell them, "It's not I aren't, what should it be?" They looked at me pityingly and replied. "Well, it isn't I isn't!" John used to roar with laughter. "It's a good job you taught me English so well," he'd say.

They were lovely children to work with from a wide variety of families. Wealthier parents were in the wool trade or land-owning farmers. Others were agricultural workers. The lime works was also a big employer and paid better than teaching, so that every September I'd hear of the foreign holidays enjoyed by the children of these workers when I had been little further than Lancashire. There were the usual arguments, as now, about taking children out of school in term time. "My dad says we can," I'd hear, and there was little I could do.

Threshfield is one of the oldest schools in continual use in the country. Three centuries ago, all the children were boarders, with the headmaster living above the porch. Being so old, our building was reputed to have a ghost, Pam the Fiddler.

Once the boys were in bed, the headmaster would go out into the playground and play his fiddle to soothe them to sleep. The local rector strode up and ordered him to stop, saying the music was going straight to the devil. They fought and the schoolmaster was killed. In our playground we could still see the large stone beneath which the body was said to have been hidden afterwards.

Late in the evenings, as I was working alone in the school, the children would see lights on and the following morning, their solemn faces full of dread, would tell me Pam the Fiddler had been in the school. Listening to them in equal solemnity, I would eventually enlighten them. "It wasn't Pam the Fiddler, it was Ivy Starkie."

One night a man staggered past the school, much the worse for wear, and on seeing the lights decided it was Pam the Fiddler and jumped into a nearby spring known as Ladywell, which was supposed to have holy power, and stayed there until morning in its protection. I bet his wife gave him a good walloping. But this was all part of the joy of country life, that stories were carried down the generations.

Despite being such a small and isolated establishment,

our long history caught the attention of Play School, the BBC children's programme, in the mid to late 1960s. Johnny Ball was the lively presenter and the crew decided that a group of my pupils would make model boats and sail them down on the River Wharfe nearby. "I know what's going to happen here," I thought, but kept my misgivings to myself.

Leaning over the bridge, I watched as the children, babbling in excitement, argued with the TV crew. Familiar with the tides and eddies of their river, they warned, "You can't do that, they'll sink!" But our glamorous visitors thought they knew better, insisting the shot went ahead, only to see the little craft sink. I told them, "These country children know what's what."

We had only just started serving school dinners then. Previously, the children had to either go home or bring a snack. This meal was sacrosanct and I insisted that our boating trip concluded before dinner time. But being the BBC, they had booked into the best hotel around, the Wilson Arms in Grassington, and took me and the children over there for lunch. Sitting in the smart dining room, watching the children swinging their legs as they sat on the polished chairs, I kept fingers crossed they would behave. I need not have worried.

One, whose family kept a dairy farm, turned to me later and said, in an awed whisper, "We've got cream in our coffee!"

"Yes," I replied, "that's what you get in nice hotels."

"We don't get any cream at home. It all goes to the Milk Marketing Board," he informed me.

After our sumptuous meal, I was guiding my charges out of the hotel's grand doorway when a Land Rover screeched to a halt on the road nearby. It was Tant Dean (the local name for Anthony), chairman of the school managers, as they were called before the system of governors was brought in. "What the bloody hell's going on here?" he demanded. They don't mix their language in The Dales.

"What do you mean?" I said, coolly, the children frozen into statues.

"Headmistress and pupils coming out of a pub at lunchtime!" he roared. It was all bluster on his part, of course.

"Don't you think it's a good idea?" I asked, calmly. "This is all in the way of education. They've all had a lovely three course meal."

Tant and I got on well once we had the measure of each other. At Christmas he would bring in a bottle of sherry, ordering me, "Send them all out to play!" and he, my assistant and I would toast the season out of water tumblers as the children peered in on us through the windows.

He still rings me up from time to time. "Na then, Ivy, how's it going?" he says, and it's lovely. They still think well of me in Yorkshire and I count Tant and his wife Phyllis amongst my dearest friends. We are still in contact after all these years.

Selecting who should take part in the programme had been too flammable a task for me, for such a decision is never forgotten nor forgiven if in the negative. During assembly, in sailed this exotic team from the BBC, typically scruffy in their leather jackets and jeans, in stark contrast to the simple cottons and woollens worn by my country children.

I think it was the producer who did most of the talking. I don't think he got out of London much. "We're in the country here, how many of you keep cows?" he asked the sea of little faces upturned towards him. A few hands straggled up for that. "How many keep bulls?" was the next question. No hands.

"What, nobody keeps bulls?" was the city man's astonished reply.

I didn't like the way this was going. A lovely lad called John Stephenson stood up and said, "You don't want to be keeping a bull all winter."

"Oh, why not?"

"It eats its head off all winter. We keep the A.I. man, it's a lot cheaper!"

How often I used to wish the floor would open up and drop me in! To my further dismay, the producer turned to me, a quizzical look on his face. "A.I. man? What's that?" I intervened swiftly and told him to ask me later, mentally wording a discreet explanation of artificial insemination for this city boy.

As if nothing worse could happen, I spotted John on his feet again. "And if it doesn't take the first time, you get the next time free," he explained.

At least the producer had the wit to select John to be on the programme. Otherwise, it was all great fun, an opening out of person to person, and that's what education is about.

In 1974 when Threshfield celebrated its tercentenary, a team from Play School returned and the first thing the producer said to me was, "Mrs Starkie, how's the A.I. man?" They brought a telescope for the school and it was a wonderful day, of which I will tell more later.

The story of the A.I. man soon spread. One day I was walking up the steep hill to my home in Grassington a mile and a half away when a car pulled up. The man inside leant out and offered me a lift. "You have the advantage of me, for I don't think I know you," I replied, slightly wary. "Yes you do," he said. "I'm the bull in the bowler hat!" That was the local nickname for the A.I. man.

"I'm glad to meet you, I've heard a lot about you!" I told him. Even today that story haunts me. Threshfield has a wonderful new extension and I am invited to the opening ceremony and am promised, "John Stephenson will be there, he'll want to talk to you about the A.I. man."

The school song, words by Ivy Starkie
music Milton Allan

By Wharfe's brave flowing waters
Where moorland greets the sun,
Our ancient school was founded
The message was begun,
As new Elizabethans
The torch we carry on,
And bring time honoured Threshfield
New honours we have won.

Chorus
Long life to our old school
Is the song we sing today,
And this our golden rule:
"Be the Best" at work and play.
From Elizabeth to Elizabeth
Three hundred years and more,
May our school go marching on
And live three hundred more.

Chapter Eight

Geese, Bats and Other School Visitors

During my 25 years as a village school headmistress, I was often asked why I hid myself away somewhere so remote, which was how some people viewed it. For me, it was the intense personal involvement I had with my pupils and the community which made it so special and gave me direct opportunities to make a difference.

I was also lucky to be teaching at a time when we had flexibility to respond to the particular needs of our children and go off on a tangent now and again, if we thought they could benefit from such a diversion. Today everything is the same across the country and there is little freedom to explore unexpected thoughts or events.

Even then, however, we dreaded the arrival of the county advisor. A billowing cloak flapping around her in the wind, she would sail in like a witch and she was absolutely awful, lacking the true love of teaching which is so essential. At one point, chanting the times-tables went out of fashion but I considered this a basic skill to be learned and continued to teach them, discretely.

My desk was near the window and if I saw her car pull up outside, we'd put the tables away quickly and get out whatever the latest mathematical fad was. One fine day she swooped down and asked why the children weren't out in the fields, to which one of the more friendly farmers allowed us access. It was at a time when I was in sole charge of all 35 pupils and I explained that I couldn't take out the whole lot of them.

"Then send out some on their own," she commented.

I knew just what would happen if I did. They would be scrambling over high walls and looking for big stones to smash in the hope of finding fossils. "There is no phone here," I pointed out, "and it is 10 miles to the nearest hospital if one of them breaks a leg. I cannot send them out unsupervised." She wasn't happy but she went away, so that was alright.

On another occasion she said I should get some livestock for the school. I thought, "I've got enough livestock sat in front of me." To show willing, I put the problem to my assistant. She knew someone who could supply some geese which, she pointed out, would crop our grass, avoiding the need for mowing. "That's a good idea," I thought, and we settled on some Chinese geese with a black stripe round the head to be a bit different.

After school one day we set off with some empty sacks, our heads equally empty of any knowledge about geese whatsoever. Travelling back with the geese in their sacks on the back seat, I was visualising the children drawing these beautiful animals. Two minutes after being released into the playground, they raised their heads, caught the scent of the stream which led down to the river and sailed away into the night, never to be seen again. I was furious because we'd paid quite a lot for them.

The following September, I set off to organise our regular display of work at the Kilnsey Show, a lovely big agricultural event tucked beneath the imposing slab of Kilnsey Crag. John had given me a lift up there with all the children's paintings and then gone off to work. I wasn't sure how I'd get back to school but assumed something would turn up.

After hanging our paintings, I wandered into the produce tent and there, bold as brass, was a plate labelled, "Chinese Goose Eggs". Gingerly, I turned the plate over to see who had entered this exotic display and discovered the name of the farmer who had been adopted by our geese. I could hardly accuse him, so that was the end of the livestock episode.

If I felt something was wrong, I considered it my duty to speak up. In the 1960s, I was in the National Association for the Teaching of English, attending meetings in London to consider the Plowden Report into education.

New methods of teaching reading were being put forward with which I disagreed profoundly. It was a quick and easy way for children to read but did not prepare them for the more complex material they would need to decipher by the age of 10 and I made my views known.

Another thorn in my side was the PE advisor. To my country children, running, climbing and swimming came as naturally as walking. They didn't need exercises to teach them how to balance. One day, we were just setting off for Linton Falls nearby when the advisor arrived to see if we were doing the kind of circus tricks with balls and beanbags which she considered essential.

"Come with us," I said, "I'll show you something." At the stepping stones, where the river bounced and squeezed its way through, she watched in awe as the older children leapt with ease from one slippery slab to the next. "You see?" I pointed out. "They don't need to be taught how to balance."

She could only agree. Meanwhile, the little ones had made a dam between two of the steps to create a pool in which they made a fearsome collection of fat crayfish. When the time came to leave, they begged, "Can't we take them back to school?" No, they could not. This PE advisor came again and envied our outdoor lesson on the River Wharfe, so she must have been satisfied.

If I hadn't loved Nature and the countryside, I couldn't have enjoyed my job there. You have to explore what the potential is. That's what teaching is, you draw from the children what they need and you give them back what you have.

Mostly I was well content with my little empire. I had had a brief experience of a much bigger, busier school. Towards the end of the war, I worked at Peel Park Primary, which is next to Accrington Stanley football ground. Some teachers love that kind of busy environment and might view village school life as claustrophobic but I disliked the hurly burly of it intensely. Bells would herald the end of lessons and it was just like Crewe Station.

One funny incident which sticks in my mind from that period in Accrington is of a young man peering through my classroom window to find his son. I opened the door and asked him naively, "Are you the father of one of my children?"

"No, but I'd like to be!" he said, with a twinkle in his eye. I didn't make that mistake twice.

The main sport in the village of Threshfield was rugby for we had a very successful club in Upper Wharfedale, who had an all-England player, and most of the children loved it. However, I knew little about the sport and so for my pupils it was football. In those days parents would waltz into school unannounced and unchallenged. One irate father came blinding in, demanding, "Where the bloody hell's the headmistress?" I told him to sit down.

"You're teaching him to play with the wrong shaped ball!" he told me.

"The wrong shaped ball?" I inquired.

"He's to play rugby, I don't want him playing with a round ball!"

"I'm awfully sorry but when I trained to teach it was rounders and cricket but if he wants to bring a different-shaped ball he can have it in the playground."

That was communication and compromise, which I promoted at every turn.

I will write later of my work with the women's movement but when I had the opportunity to use my international contacts to benefit the school, I did so. I wanted to make sure the children met as wide a variety of people as possible. Consequently, we had visits from Jamaica, Haiti and many other places. My Haitian guests spoke French so the children learned in advance to say "hello" and "how are you". The replies came in a torrent of French and the children looked at me for help, but I hadn't followed it either.

Being a headmistress meant having many roles to play, including being a staff manager and a diplomat. In many ways, the most important relationship she can have is not with the pupils or the parents or even the managers but with the caretaker. If you don't get on, there's constant trouble.

However, I was fortunate in my caretakers. One, a woman, would arrive at four o' clock on the dot every day and sweep towards my desk where I would be marking books or doing paperwork. On arriving beside me, she would hang on the end of the brush and tell me all that was going on. She was better than The News of The World. She was a lovely person and wrote me a very nice letter when I left, thanking me for all I had done.

She was also psychic. To get to know the children better when I first arrived, I set them a project to do their family trees, asking them to find photos of their parents and grandparents. On this particular afternoon, my own family photos, which I had brought in to inspire them, were scattered across the desk. This lady stopped and pointed to one. "That man is in this school," she announced. It was a picture of my grandfather, still keeping a critical eye on me, no doubt.

"He can't be, he's dead!" I protested.

"I don't care, he's in this school. It means you're going to be alright."

It was a comforting thought.

I had a strong sense of the history of my school and you could feel an atmosphere but to me it was only the footprints of the hundreds of children who had passed that way.

My caretaker believed otherwise and John warned me not to laugh at what was obviously a genuine feeling that she had. For my part, I experienced only one disconcerting moment when, alone in the building, a door closed for no apparent reason. John advised, "If it's Pam the Fiddler, tell him you play the violin too!" But no other opportunity arose to do so. I took it all with a pinch of salt.

With such a sense of the past, I often met opposition to change and had to take a stand. When I started to organise parents' evenings, I was told no-one would come after dark for there were no streetlights and the school was haunted. Eventually people did come but I had to wait for better weather and lighter nights. Being a rural school, we had to get along with the local farmers and occasionally one would be particularly trying. Sheep were always escaping and getting into our yard, which we accepted as part of country life. I'd get big Leslie, the lad I'd converted by addressing him with, "Na then!" and he'd get them back into the field in no time. He loved that job. We had no idea to which farmer the animals belonged but did the best we could.

One day after an interruption of this kind, an irate farmer burst into the school - no knocking on doors - demanding to know, "Where's the silly b***er who's put my sheep out of the way?"

I stood my ground. "It's a farmer's duty to fence his stock. We have done the best we could," I told him.

He sloped off, grumbling. Some time later, a brand new, bright yellow car drew up outside and out stepped the school meals organiser from Wakefield. After talking to the kitchen staff, she returned to me deeply upset. "Just look at my car!" she wailed.

I went out with her to see the beautiful yellow car covered in slurry. Our unfriendly farmer had driven past with his muck spreader and, instead of turning it off while in the lane, had kept the spray on. He was getting his own back and presumably thought the car belonged to me.

It was big Leslie to the rescue again who, with another boy, sloshed buckets of water over the car and restored its yellow glow once more.

Though I loved the historic atmosphere of my school, it held back progress at times as it was a listed building and all alterations had to be in keeping. Our roof leaked, requiring buckets to be placed on the floor, just waiting for small feet to kick them over accidentally. I lost count of the number of times that was on the agenda at our managers' meetings. Tant Dean, chairman of the managers, and I got on very well. On first meeting him, I was in fear and trembling because I had been warned he was a shocker but he turned out to be my Heathcliffe, with dark, wavy hair and a strong character. He was our school's champion and was very forthright. At one meeting, he slammed his fist on the table and told the council representatives present, "Get that bloody roof fixed!"

I recoiled in shock, not at the language which I privately endorsed under the circumstances, but out of respect for the Rector, who was also present, and warned Tant to mind his words.

"I don't care! Get that bloody roof fixed!" he repeated.

Bats discovered the gaps between the stone slab tiles and set up home in our roof, then began to explore the classrooms. No sooner had we served the dinners than their little black shapes would swoop down to investigate. I didn't like it and the children, despite knowing all about bats, were scared of them. I already had chalk in my hair, I didn't want bats as well.

From the council came an expert who said we couldn't do anything as bats were a protected species, even if they are dive-bombing school dinners. Watching their antics with interest, he said, "They shouldn't be out in the daytime." It was scant comfort for us.

When at last the bats left and someone found some money in the council purse to do our roof, it was such a big job that we were shunted up the road temporarily to the new secondary school nearby where we squatted in the youth wing, as it was known. We lived out of cardboard boxes for I don't know how long.

Inevitably there was friction. My little girls and boys

were faced with the daunting journey to the senior toilets where much larger and, at times, more threatening children were often hanging around. My pupils either daren't go in or they daren't come out. Like a tigress protecting her cubs, I'd go banging into the boys toilets, oblivious to the enraged expressions on the faces of these teenagers, and demand they stop bullying my children.

On hearing of this, the headmaster of the secondary school told me, "You shouldn't be in there, Mrs Starkie!"

"Tell me, then, how I am going to avoid it?" I retorted. "My children have to use those toilets!" It wasn't easy and it was with great happiness that we eventually returned to our dry, bat-free village school.

To me the only change in the atmosphere was from damp to dry but our caretaker stood gazing round her, sensing something else. "It's not the same," she told me.

I was jolly glad it wasn't the same but she wasn't talking about the absence of buckets. "They've let Pam the Fiddler out," she said.

For the first few years of my headship at Threshfield, Tim was one of my pupils. When the time came for the 11-plus exam, which would determine what kind of secondary education a child received, I was not allowed to have any contact with the exam papers. They were all delivered instead to the home of my assistant teacher and, when the time of the exams came, I would to go to a different school to invigilate.

Tim did so well that I worried people might suspect I had found some way round this security but it was all through his own hard work.

We decided to send him to boarding school near Bradford, though at first I didn't want him to go away. But

John was adamant that Tim would get on faster without me urging him always to do better. It broke my heart but was probably for the best. The night before he left I was up late washing, ironing and labelling his clothes before laying them neatly in his trunk. The matron told Tim his was the best packed trunk she'd ever seen.

From then on during term time we saw him only every three weeks when they had a day off and we would drive over to bring Tim home. I'd feed him up, because he was always hungry, then press all his clothes.

My plan had been to move on to some more glittering post once Tim was on his way but I didn't and have never regretted my decision. One of the highlights of my time at Threshfield was the tercentenary of the school in 1974, a memorable day preceded by a marathon of organisation.

Sitting at a meeting of parents who had offered to help, there was talk of "buttering scones" and so on. I knew our event, to which many past pupils, staff and dignitaries would be invited, needed more. "We'll have to have outside caterers," I announced, firmly. A shocked silence filled the room. Outside caterers? You can imagine how that went down in Yorkshire. However, I got that through.

Our hall wasn't big enough for such a crowd and in any case I wanted it to be an exhibition area showing the work of the school, past and present, and I ordered a marquee. We turned all preparations into a learning experience for the children who watched in fascination as this huge tent rose up to fill almost the entire yard.

From the admissions register, I did my best to contact every former pupil who might still be alive. I insisted on proper printed invitations with a tear-off reply slip and had to fight every inch of the way for things like that. "I'll ask him, he'll come," I'd be told but I knew that such informal organisation could plunge our event into chaos. It was headmistress versus village but in the end it was such a huge success they forgot that it hadn't all been their idea.

Threshfield had been founded as a grammar school by the Rev. Matthew Hewitt in 1674. The Hewitt Trust was still in existence, representatives sat on our board of managers and the trust contributed towards the cost of our celebrations. Another result of this connection was the arrival of American descendants of Hewitt to join in with our day and they spent a fortnight at the Wilson Arms in Grassington, returning home with a painting of the school done by a local artist. We raised funds by selling further paintings of Threshfield and souvenir mugs.

In the end there were about 200 guests, the oldest of whom was 90. I insisted that the top person in county education attended, so we got Lord Masham of Swinton Hall who was chairman of primary education and was our main speaker.

At last the big day arrived, June at its hottest and sunniest, and I stood before the mirror to put on the big hat I felt appropriate. Celebrations were to start at 2.30pm, preceded by lunch at the Wilson Arms for the VIPs, who included the Bishop of Bradford.

John was there of course and Tim with his wife Maureen and I roped them all into helping to put labels on the chairs. Because the local policeman's children were my pupils, the road was closed off for us and parking organised by Sgt Gains.

Meanwhile, Lord Masham was lost among the winding lanes of Upper Wharfedale. Stopping a man to ask the way, he became impatient with the lengthy directions,

The tercentenary. Front: John Dean (brother of Tant), Ivy, the Bishop of Bradford, Lord Masham. Back: John Starkie, Mrs Barlow, Canon Barlow (rector), Mrs John Dean.

Threshfield School tercentenary celebration programme

WOODCUT BY D. WHITEHEAD

𝕿𝖍𝖗𝖊𝖘𝖍𝖋𝖎𝖊𝖑𝖉 𝕻𝖗𝖎𝖒𝖆𝖗𝖞 𝖘𝖈𝖍𝖔𝖔𝖑
𝕿𝖊𝖗𝖈𝖊𝖓𝖙𝖊𝖓𝖆𝖗𝖞 𝕮𝖊𝖑𝖊𝖇𝖗𝖆𝖙𝖎𝖔𝖓𝖘

𝕾𝖆𝖙𝖚𝖗𝖉𝖆𝖞, 𝕸𝖆𝖞 18𝖙𝖍. 1974 𝖆𝖙 2𝖕𝖒

interrupting with, "Hurry up, my man, I'm Lord Masham and I'm late for an important event!"

To which the reply was, "And I'm Lord Nelson!" However, he made it and the day was an enormous success until the heavy heat sparked a thunderstorm. Our country school had little in the way of proper drainage and our playground relied on a small soakaway to cope with excess water. Sitting on the platform, I could see straight down the main aisle towards this drain, to which, mercifully, most people had their backs turned. I nudged Lord Masham discretely. "I don't know how long you're planning to speak for but hurry up or we'll all be under water!"

We wound things up swiftly before the flood came in, tactfully abbreviating our oldest guest of 90 who, despite not being in the programme, was determined to make his own speech, and ushered everyone into the main school building. Lord Masham found it all highly amusing. "I've been to some very grand do's in huge halls which have been rather fuddy-duddy and boring," he told me, "but I've enjoyed every minute of this."

We sang the school song, which I had written, and nobody was in a hurry to leave. It was a lovely day and I enjoyed it all. At the end, my daughter-in-law, who is also a teacher and often felt I was hiding my light under the bushel that was Threshfield, said, "I can see why you like country schools. This is teaching with the lid off."

Over my time there, I saw subtle changes in the children as more cars meant more travel and better job opportunities emerged. Gradually they gave more application to their work as they saw a wider future than farm labouring or lime making. I worked them hard and trained them like racehorses, getting six or seven each year into the grammar school in Skipton.Though each was coaxed to their full potential, some would never excel academically, but try telling that to the parents! One particular mother produced a child a year to add to my roll. After registering one who had arrived particularly late on in her child-bearing career, she said to me, "Mrs Starkie, I didn't intend to have another. I thought I was round the Cape of Good Hope and I wasn't."

Adding this new phrase to my ever-expanding vocabulary, I heard her go on. "He's going to be the last, so I'd like him to get to the grammar school."

By now I was expert at showing no emotion in my face but behind the mask came the thought, "He couldn't catch a bus at a bus-stop!" but I reassured her I would do my best for her son, as for all my young charges.

Most of the parents were good, genuine folk and she was no exception. Her life was busy and hard but if there was a health visitor to be seen at the school, she would always have her hair done for the occasion, which made me smile.

When the time came for the child to prepare for the 11-plus exam, his mother insisted he be given homework and I couldn't say no, however doomed was this hope. After a few days she returned with a resigned look on her face, "Mrs Starkie, this homework - even I can't do it." And the mask thought, "There you are, love, there's your answer." But she wanted the best for her children and I respected her feelings. As she left, she turned and confided, "He doesn't want to go to the grammar school anyway because they don't play football, only rugby."

Chapter Nine

Working for Equality

My life fell into three compartments - private, professional and public. In our free time, especially when Tim was back from the boarding school, the three of us liked to go out exploring. John was honing his photography skills, going to college in his spare time to study for his MRPS (Member of the Royal Photographic Society). Landscape photography was his passion. He presented me with a small camera of my own which he said was idiot-proof. I proved him wrong.

Leisure time was precious because, like all working women, I would finish on a Friday and go straight home to do my housework. At first, I was the only working wife in my part of Grassington.

The teacher who had been at Threshfield before me lived nearby. One Friday, as I was scraping the ash out of the fire grate, wearing a headscarf round my hair and looking awful, she swept in wearing a big hat and informed me, "I was at Threshfield School for many years and on a Friday I used to cry, because we were leaving it until Monday."

John was a good cook. He could stew a dishcloth and make a meal of it. I did the apple pies and the custards. Before we married, my mother warned him, "You know these school teachers, they can't boil water," to which he replied, "Don't worry, I can."

One dramatic event which caused a stir in our village was the arrival of Prince Charles who landed in a helicopter in the field next-door on his way to open a new fell rescue centre. There were so many of us lined up behind my garden wall that he came over to chat. He had a red rose in his button hole, so I told him, "You're wearing the wrong colour rose!" And he replied, "I know, it should be white for Yorkshire."

My professional life as a teacher took up much of my time but, in addition to that, I also began work with a women's organisation which was to have a profound impact on my life and which contributed to changes in the way women are treated in the workplace.

Preparing for this book, I found myself surrounded by papers, minutes of meetings and reports from which I have selected some anecdotes which I hope will give readers a snapshot of what life was like. All this work was done voluntarily and through a sense of service. My expenses were paid, if I was lucky.

To give a brief overview, I was active for many years in the United Kingdom Federation of Business and Professional Women (now Business and Professional Women UK) and am still a member. The organisation exists to bring together working women and to carry their voice to national attention on important issues affecting women. I also became part of the international links between the B&P and similar organisations across the world.

As I became well known in public life, I later found myself on a quango working towards equal pay for women.

In addition to all this, John and I also set up an

international organisation to bring together the many people living in our home area who had come from abroad.

In the late 1950s, I took the first steps into this public life which would bring both John and I into contact with many interesting people and take us around Britain and also abroad.

We had remained in contact with the Spencer family and it was Mrs Spencer who started me on this new path. She was a member of the Burnley branch of the B&P and asked me to speak there, then suggested I join.

I was very interested because, much as I loved working in a village school, I felt it was important to stretch myself so that I had more to offer my pupils. It's not enough to get them to sit up straight if there's nothing else going on. They will be living in tomorrow's world and you've got to be on the ball.

Burnley was too far from my home, so in 1958 I was a founder member of the Skipton and District club. Our launch event was a very smart do at a hotel opposite Skipton railway station and we were supported by Burnley members, who had sponsored us. On our big night, we watched the delegation from Burnley picking their way across the road in their long dresses and high heels. We went from strength to strength and I went on to become national president.

My marriage to John had made me acutely aware of the strength and support needed by those from abroad trying to make a new life in Britain, so we also set up a separate international club for both men and women in the area. It was surprising how many people had ended up Yorkshire after starting life in other parts of the world.

I also encouraged international links through Business

Ivy with Mrs Spencer (left) at a B&P dinner in Burnley, March 1969, when Ivy was Yorkshire Divisional Chairman

A B&P dinner in Blackburn where John was guest speaker (back row, centre)

and Professional Women. Every year the B&P had an international night at which we would light a candle for each of the countries with which we had links. John would come with me. Some countries, like Poland, were now shut off from us by the Iron Curtain and their candles would remain symbolically unlit. It was a moving moment for us both when those candles were eventually lit once again.

The event was held in February, which is fine if you're in South Africa but in Skipton it snowed. On the way back up the dale, the snow was blowing straight at our car, in the back seat of which were packed three Spaniards who worked at a local hotel. One leant over and said, "Never mind, you gave a very nice talk!"

At the bottom of the hill before Grassington, a policeman stopped us. "This road has been closed since six o'clock!" he said. We looked at each other in astonishment. Closed? We'd just come up it! John's theory in snow was to just keep driving, not change gear or anything. When we finally reached home, I asked myself why I was doing all this.

In 1965 I was given an international award of £60 to attend a week-long conference in Geneva of the ILO, (International Labour Organisation, labour meaning employment rather than political) which was held at the United Nations headquarters. The subject was "The Employment of Women With Family Responsibilities" which was just up my street. John and I went on the ferry from Hull to Rotterdam and drove down to Switzerland.

John had a pass and was able to listen to the debates. He was an enormous help to me with his wide knowledge of languages, when he wasn't out with his camera. He enjoyed meeting so many people. The conference hall was a swirl of colours as all the others were in their national costume. There was I in my twin-set and pearls. I sat next to a university lecturer from the Sudan who was wearing a gorgeous outfit which fell in folds around her. She told me, "In my country, if a woman does not go back to work the day after she has had her baby, her husband will beat her." I couldn't believe this was happening in the 20th century. It put our struggles for equality in Britain into perspective.

I scattered invitations all round to visit me in Grassington before we wound our way slowly back to Yorkshire. On arrival, I had a message from Mr Ebo of Lagos, Nigeria, with whom I had been friendly. "I am at Leeds Bradford Airport, I will wait for you."

We picked him up and brought him back to the village where his beautiful tunic and cap caused quite a sensation. It was very nice to see him but a bit worrying. His aim was Oxford University, to which I said I was unlikely to be able to even get him past the gate. After staying with us for a while, he went on his way.

A woman in a fabulous turban arrived after another international congress at which she had announced simply, "I am coming to stay with you" and she did.

John and I had the disquieting experience of watching delegates from Poland and the Soviet Union attend these conferences. We knew they were not free to say what they liked, as we were, and their main aim was more likely to be reporting back what others were saying. John said, "You can pick them out" and he was right, for they all stuck together and had been dressed for the event, the women in identical white court shoes. Consequently he had little to do with them.

As a result of my international work, I was invited to

St. James's Palace to meet the Duke of Edinburgh over afternoon cocktails for which I wore a navy suit and matching hat. John accompanied me to London but unfortunately was not invited to the palace. Some of the other women had been to a beauty parlour to have their make-up done. I'd put mine on in the train. To my surprise, the Duke of Edinburgh also had make-up on, that sort of tan they have for television, and that quite upset me.

He asked me about my international group and asked me if the council funded us, to which I replied that we raised funds ourselves. "Go back and sack the council," he said, "don't put up with that." So when I returned to Skipton I was able to approach the council and say, "I have a message for you from the Duke of Edinburgh that I've to sack you."

Slowly, the work I and many others were doing to improve the lot of working women was gaining recognition. In those days, there was no maternity leave and some were even told to leave their jobs on marriage.

I began to campaign for equal pay for equal work, which was a two-edged sword involving the responsibility of doing that equal work. The Women's National Commission was a quango with which I became involved looking at legislation affecting women.

Endless arguments ensued as some women said they couldn't do an equal job because of their domestic responsibilities and my view was, "If we can't do it, we can't ask for equal pay." I also pointed out that if women could receive the State pension at 60, men should be able to. Of course it has gone the other way with women receiving it later but at least it's more fair.

In 1968, with a Government Green Paper on equal

pay called Justice or Prejudice in my hands, fresh in that morning's post, I set off for a television studio in Leeds to speak on the six o'clock news. After being welcomed by the studio staff, they seemed relieved that I could indeed talk, which anyone can discover after two minutes with me. Then the presenters, all men then, went off to change their shirts to blue ones, which look better on camera, and spent ages doing their hair.

I often raced from school down to the studio to speak on this and that. John would sit at home to watch me and in many of my pupils' homes the TV would be on to watch Mrs Starkie. I got to see how things worked behind the scenes and on one occasion mild panic broke out when it was discovered that the weather forecast hadn't arrived, so the presenters made it up.

At that time women faced appalling discrimination at which today's killer-heel wearing career girls would blanche. Married women did not have equality in law with their husbands and had no automatic guardianship of their children. Since then we have come a long way.

I welcomed arguments over policy but not petty personal fallings out. One evening I went all the way to Weston-super-Mare and was due back to work the next morning. Two women were involved in a petty and spiteful vendetta and I could have banged their heads together. In Scarborough where they were all falling out I suggested forming separate clubs, which they did. But overall I found the work satisfying, despite travelling the night hours on many occasions.

As first vice-chairman and then chairman of the Yorkshire region, I had 45 clubs and visited them all. For all my public work, including serving on the quango, I received only my train fare and the cost of staying in a modest hotel, though mostly I drove home.

I had an aversion to staying with people I hardly knew. One woman put me up for the night, saying, "I don't have breakfast but there are some stewed prunes if you'd like them." I had to get an early train back to Leeds and wasn't going to risk eating prunes beforehand. I never went there again.

As a young boy, Tim got used to hearing me say that I was going out to "take the chair" at various different places and was rather puzzled by this. Consequently, when anyone asked him what his mother did, Tim would reply, "She takes chairs," and leave them wondering if I worked in a furniture shop.

I have sat on many chairs at meetings but on only one occasion have I ended up with that chair in my home. I have a swivel chair in my lounge today which came from Skipton council chamber. The chairman of the council had to speak to my members and was nervous about what to say, so I gave him some tips, for which he was grateful. "Just be yourself," I said to him. Much later, when the council chamber was refurbished, he presented me with two lovely chairs which were no longer needed.

Professional toastmasters were the opposition as far as I was concerned, for their ethos was not about being natural. After a long journey to Evesham in Worcestershire, I gave my speech, after which the toastmaster said to me, rather condescendingly, "You were rather nervous, weren't you?"

"No, not really."

"I think you were. I was watching you and you kept putting your shoe on and off."

"That's because it hurt!" I informed him.

Invited to a civic dinner at Hull, I wore a cocktail dress with ostrich feathers round the hem - Shirley Bassey wasn't in it! Sitting next to the mayor at dinner, he astonished me by saying, "I bet those feathers keep your neck warm!" What are you supposed to do in a situation like that with everyone out front looking at you?

Things went from bad to worse. The mayor leant over and the silver medallion fell from his chain and rolled on to the floor. There we were, the mayor and I, scrabbling around under the table looking for it in full view of all the other guests. Afterwards, my B&P ladies asked me, "What were you doing under the table with the mayor?" to which I replied, "Never you mind but I'd rather not have been doing it."

Leaving Hull, we took a wrong turning and were eventually flagged down by a policeman near the docks. There I was, sitting in my long dress, fur stole and my chain of office. "What are you doing down here at this time of night," he wanted to know. I opened my coat, flashed my chain and said, "I've just been to a very important occasion with the mayor." He put us on the right road.

You never knew what was going to happen. Up in the Dales, a huge black dog was said to roam the moors at night. At five o'clock one morning, John and I were driving to Leeds for the seven o'clock train, crossing open moorland, when suddenly there was a bump on the front of the car. John said, "I must have bent the number plate on something" and stopped to look but there was nothing there at all. So that must have been the mysterious black dog.

On another occasion, a dinner was held in a public swimming baths covered over temporarily with a wooden floor. The heater to warm the water below us remained on and through the evening it got hotter and hotter.

I've had some terrible journeys. Setting off in the snow, I'd hitch my long dress up round my waist, put on a coat and sheepskin boots and trudge off to the car. Of course one night I forgot to take any shoes with me and spent the evening looking beautiful in my long dress and a pair of bedroom slippers which someone found for me.

I have to be thankful to Philip's mother for guiding me into this public work. Also, in these later years, Philip's brother Ken had grown up into an academic, now an MA and Msc. Ken Spencer is an archivist, historian and writer. We keep in contact, now in our eighties, and have a lot in common. I am sure Philip would be pleased to know our lives have continued like this.

Chapter Ten

Politicians and Palaces

I was on the National Executive for about 12 years, which meant dashing up and down to London. I became National Vice President and then National President in 1975, serving a two-year term, and my public life took me within the orbit of many famous - and infamous - people.

The phone rang at school one day and it was Paul Raymond, who had made a fortune from pornographic magazines and strip clubs. There was me, in the middle of maths and milk bottles, squeezed into the stockroom where the telephone was, talking to Paul Raymond.

He wanted to know what I thought of Germaine Greer, the author causing a stir with her feminist books. I told him that some of the sexual gyrations she talked about were physically impossible. I'm still not quite sure why he rang me. I think he was just out to do feminism down and I suppose wanted to quote me in a magazine. He was trying me out and I thought, "He's not going to win on this."

To me, the beatings and suppression suffered by some women in Africa were far more serious problems for us to be considering and we worked hard for their benefit as well as banging the drum for equality in Britain. I was concerned that strident feminists were in danger of making

Ivy on becoming National President of the B&P in 1975 and (below) her acceptance speech

FIRSTLY, may I say thank you for electing me as your President. This is an overwhelming honour, not undertaken lightly. The task of responsible leadership, at any level, in any organisation, requires total commitment. This I will endeavour to give to every member, to the Federation as an organisation and to the furtherance of our aims. As I take office, I take heart from all the messages of good will and offers of help I have received. What a wonderful spirit of unity prevails within our Federation and what a tremendous force this could be if we could channel such united efforts to achieve our objectives!

No President could have a greater challenge, or greater opportunity to prove her worth than in International Women's Year. There is no need to stress this is the 'year of the woman'. At Government level one woman has already made a tremendous breakthrough but let us not become complacent. We need to assess our resources to question our abilities to prove our worth and accept the responsibility which goes with our hard-earned equality.

1975 is a year of challenge to every woman. Ovid once remarked that 'What one sees of a woman is the least part of her'. In this special year, offering full global attention to the role and social position of women, what the world sees of us must be the very best we can offer.

I hope many of you will have already become involved, on steering committees, organising projects, participating in united efforts in your town and community, to show society the total potential of women.

Recently in an interview I was asked 'Are you the ones who light candles?' Is this the only way our Federation can get publicity? This year let us not only light candles but blaze torches and make a real bonfire of prejudice as we achieve full equality.

I look forward to a happy working partnership with you all.

Joy Starkie

112

all of us appear cranks. More pleasant to meet were some of the celebrity speakers at meetings of the B&P, including the naturalist David Bellamy, and Russell Braddon, who had written a book, The Naked Island, about his experiences as a Japanese prisoner-of-war. Russell Braddon, on hearing that John had also been a prisoner-of-war, asked what was wrong with him.

"Why do you ask that?" I replied.

"Because if he has been a PoW, it will be either his stomach or his heart." He was right, of course.

Another guest was the sister of the round-the-world sailor Robin Knox Johnston. At the time of her visit, he was still on his solo trip. She confided, "I'm very worried about him" but I'm ashamed to say that we hadn't noticed at the time the magnificent feat being undertaken.

On a darker note, Ronald Gregory, Chief Constable of Yorkshire who handled investigations which led to the arrest of serial killer Peter Sutcliffe, was a speaker at Keighley. After sitting next to him all evening, I faced a long, dark drive home across the moors, my mind full of shadows.

In the late 1960s when I was on the Women's National Commission, the chairman was Barbara Castle, a left wing politician who had grown up in Yorkshire. She was smashing and a very good chairman who got things done. The Elizabeth Garrett Anderson Hospital in London, which was for women, was to be closed and its services transferred to The Royal Free. An unexpected by-product of this was the loss of training places for women doctors at a time when men were often given preference at mixed establishments.

We met in the Commons and, on hearing this problem, Barbara Castle asked, "Is the Health Minister in the House?

With former prisoner-of-war Russell Braddon, 1968

Fetch him!" Dr David Owen was brought before us and agreed there would be some guaranteed training places for women. Women had a direct route to policy for the first time. I was lucky to work with many people at the top who were straightforward and easy to talk to. Backing up the Commission's work was the ever-present Shirley Williams, another prominent Labour Party MP, whose clarity of thought helped push through many improvements.

As a teacher, I received less than a man doing the same job. We hadn't been brought up to fight it but at last things were beginning to change and the Commission was instrumental in bringing in the Equal Pay Act of 1970. John was a great

John giving a speech at the Wilson Arms, Grassington, where we had delegates from Buenos Aires, as our International Congress was then in London. As two foreigners together, Madame Arias and John sang, "Row, row, row the boat ... "

support to me throughout my career and my public life and was proud of what I achieved, accompanying me when he could. Sometimes I'd return from London on the milk train and he'd collect me at Leeds at some grimly early hour so I could get to work. A lot of my ladies got to know him and he was liked and respected.

Conferences always generate petty complaints about hotel rooms and such like. On the opening day, I would position John at the door and say, "Just waylay anyone you think is coming for me" and he did.

As National President, I travelled to Northern Ireland at a time of bombings, shootings and riots and he wasn't very keen but I felt our members there deserved our support. To show our solidarity, we planned our national conference in the province but had to cancel at short notice because of security fears. I sat all weekend at our headquarters redoing the tickets for the new venue of the Grosvenor House Hotel in London, which was beautiful.

When Harold Wilson was Prime Minister, I was invited to 10 Downing Street. The invitation was unhelpful, "Lounge suit". I decided to wear a long dress and walked with John out of our headquarters in London to a taxi. "10 Downing Street!" we commanded. "Get off!" retorted the driver. "We really are going there!" we protested, much to the amusement of the office staff who had come out to see us off to this prestigious event.

Arriving a little early, we found ourselves milling about Downing Street in our finery with a few others. That big black door opened and we were told, "You can't come in yet, he's not home from work yet." Eventually Harold Wilson turned up and in we went. My husband loved good wood and beautiful furniture. I was chatting away, as usual, as we stood in the lofty entrance hall and looked round to see John stroking the mahogany lovingly.

A plain-clothes security officer came up and said, "I'm sorry, Sir, it's not for sale." John didn't care a hoot. "It's lovely wood," he explained. At the top of the stairs Harold Wilson and his wife Mary were waiting to greet us. On hearing we were from Grassington, he turned to Mary and said, "That's where my parents had their honeymoon." So I was in. It was obviously the place to come from.

The main room was beautiful, with more lovely furniture for John to admire. I sat down on a rather delicate chaise longue, hardly daring to move in case it broke, and Mary Wilson came to sit beside me. She was a quiet, unassuming person and very sincere and I took an immediate liking to her. I said, "You must get tired of these occasions."

She replied, "I'm used to it now but some people will try to turn it into something political whereas this is meant to be our party for you to thank you all for what you have done." Then she turned her head disdainfully, adding, "Just look at the kind of thing they do!" I followed her eyes over to a corner and who should be there but Margaret Thatcher, deep in a debate.

However, to my delight, up came Judith Hart who had by now got to the top but had never forgotten her roots. She had been my friend at school who had a clear view of where she was going. When I was organising conferences, I invited Judith to speak at York. Everyone else in the B&P was a bit nervous, wondering how to deal with a Government Minister, but I said, "Just you wait and see."

Everyone was dressed up very smartly and on their best behaviour but Judith just walked straight up to me in a very friendly and relaxed manner and said, "Hello Ivy." That's

Ivy (left) with Dame Judith Hart (right) in 1968

what education is all about - getting on with whoever you meet. We remained in touch and I was very sad when in 1991 she died of cancer.

To me, working with ordinary women up and down the country was the most important aspect of my public life but it was interesting to receive prestigious invitations because it meant our work was being recognised. I went to a Buckingham Palace Garden Party, for which the instructions were the same: "Lounge suit."

Assuming The Queen would not be wearing such, I dressed myself in a very smart outfit with a big hat. Some of the other women even had parasols.

Mrs Phillips, mother to Captain Mark Phillips, first

husband of Princess Anne, was there and wearing an outfit similar to mine, so I tried to keep out of her way. I was rather surprised to see her being herded out with the rest of us afterwards and not being asked to stay on for another cup of tea.

I was invited to speak in the glittering surroundings of the Guild Hall, London. Afterwards I was tapped on the shoulder and turned to find Jack Ashley MP. "You gave a very good speech," he said.

I was surprised, for I knew he was deaf and had been sitting behind me with no chance to lip read. "But you can't have heard me!" I replied.

"I didn't but I saw their faces," he said.

Occasionally I came across prejudice against the North among some of the London lot who thought we knew nothing, I always stood my ground. If an event was over-running and they threatened to cut out my slot, I'd say, "I've come all this way. Cut someone who's come from down the road. I'll have my seven minutes, if you don't mind."

As chairman of our International Committee in the early 1970s, I became involved with the European Parliament and for a while was taking the train to London, then flying from Heathrow every Friday night.

I had to stand up in front of all these people to speak about educational matters. They had spent a long time talking about the Baccalaureate and as a primary school head, I got rather fed up with this. I stood up and said, "You judge a tree by its root. Let's talk about education right from the beginning because that's important." They looked at me as if I shouldn't have been talking, but I said my piece.

My international work brought me into contact with many interesting characters. Stanley Burton of the

*June 1977, outside the European Parliament building
during a Women's National Commission visit,
including Dr Grace Thornton, a close friend of Ivy*

*The Berlaymont Building, headquarters,
European Commission, Brussels*

famous menswear company was a great internationalist and philanthropist who staged monthly international meetings at their Leeds headquarters, to which I received an invitation. He took me round the works where women were sewing away at Burton suits. "How do you control all these women?" I asked.

He replied, "I don't need to, I just set one against another. If one doesn't do her quota, the others will say so. They sort it out themselves.

During my public life, I became immune to glittering surroundings and focused my attention on the ordinary people swept up in these occasions. At a Woman of the Year Lunch at the Savoy Hotel in London, I spotted Hannah Hauxwell in an area roped off for VIPs. She looked smarter than when she had been discovered living a relentlessly tough life alone on a Dales farm, but was still much the same person in the glare of her unsought fame.

The other VIPs didn't know how to talk to her because they were so London-orientated and she looked a little lost. I took no notice of the ropes but stepped up to say, "Hello Hannah, I'm from Grassington," and she brightened up and beckoned me in.

Serious issues affecting women were always at the forefront of my mind. At one conference we took a vote to campaign against female circumcision, a mutilation of women carried out in some countries, for which I provided diagrams, much to the shock of some of the delegates. "Fancy showing us that!" they said in disgust. But I pointed out, "You can't vote on something you don't understand."

My work with the Women's National Commission took me to Romania to visit their equivalent organisation just before the dictator Ceausescu was executed. On arrival, our passports were taken away, which made me feel sick with apprehension. We stayed in government-controlled hotels and were watched the whole time, which gets to you. You stop talking after a while.

However, the women with whom we worked wanted change and showed us the horrific conditions in orphanages where children were crammed together with too few staff to look after their basic needs, let alone give a hug. By contrast, our official visits were restricted to smart infants schools where children dressed in uniform and everything in the garden was lovely but we knew that behind the scenes were filth and ill-health.

Many things were accepted as normal which shocked me deeply. Our translator said, almost proudly, "I've had five abortions. Every time I'm having a baby, I can have an abortion because the government needs me." It was a highly artificial world where the latest craze among the well-off was to take monkey glands for eternal youth. Two hospital staff quite plainly in their sixties or seventies claimed to be only in their thirties.

I was very glad to reclaim my passport and fly home, much to John's relief, for he had a healthy scepticism about dictatorial regimes. Arriving back at Heathrow, we drank gallons of tea and talked and talked to get it all out of our systems.

A far more relaxed experience was a conference in Canada called Women of the World, followed by a grand tour up to the Rocky Mountains and seeing the Calgary Stampede, a massive rodeo event. For all these travels, some of my expenses were paid but others came out of my own pocket. When I went to a conference in South America in 1974, John said, "There's no good you going all the way to

International Congress in Canada, 1971, at the Banff Springs Hotel. Ivy is front row, second from the right

International Conference, Buenos Aires, 1974

Buenos Aires, Ivy, and not doing the tour."

"But it'll cost us!" I protested.

"Go on, you'll not be there again," he said, and he was right. In Rio I stayed right on Copacabana Beach and it was lovely. I'd watch children come out of school, then they would strip off their clothes and run into the sea. Afterwards they played football on the beach and flew kites. It was a long way from Threshfield.

Something that probably would not have happened back in my village home was the theft of my camera. My friend Ida Down (who had hesitated before marrying her husband because of his surname) had gone in to order lunch for us and a young man tapped me on the shoulder, saying, "Time?" As I looked at my watch, he snatched my bag containing my purse and camera. I was devastated but the hotel manager said it was hardly worth going to the police. The station was 'downtown' and I didn't fancy going there, especially since it was home to Great Train Robber Ronnie Biggs who was on the run from the British authorities.

Back in Grassington, I reported the theft to the police for my insurance claim. Our local policeman arrived on his bicycle, took out his notepad and pencil and asked, "Now Mrs Starkie, where were you robbed?" "Copacabana Beach, Rio de Janeiro," I replied, which made a change for him to record.

In my home village, my comings and goings were watched with interest. One day the postman delivered an impressive envelope, announcing, "You've got a letter from the Cabinet Office!"

"Yes," I said, would you like to read it?"

Despite all this public service, I never considered running as a councillor or MP as I wasn't a political animal.

My father was and I think that put me off, hearing him ranting on about who'd said what to whom. Life was busy but satisfying for both John and I. During all this time, John was gradually getting recognition for his professional skills, having lost all his certificates in the war. Eventually, he moved from West Riding County Council to become a surveyor/engineer for the Yorkshire Dales National Park. He also became a member of the Masons. He loved

At the Grosvenor House Hotel, London, for a meeting of the International Federation of the B&P, with Ivy as National President She is with the General Secretary, Nora Young, sister of Sir Brian Young. She had been a debutante and was a great help to Ivy with protocol.

working for the National Park, whose headquarters were close to home. They let him use the cellar of the offices as a darkroom because he was taking so many photographs. So impressed were his employers that much of his work was used in exhibitions and literature promoting the park.

Today, approaching the park boundaries, visitors see a ram's head on the National Park sign. This was John's idea. At Muker Show, he took a photo of the prize-winning ram with its huge horns and from this picture he and a designer created the original park logo.

Tim had gone to Manchester University and got an MSc in radio astronomy at Jodrell Bank, the centre for astrophysics in Cheshire, of which John and I were very proud. I took my pupils there for an outing, where the huge dish of the radio telescope thrilled them to the core. Maureen got her degree and we had yet another teacher in the family.

*The National Park emblem which came originally
from a photograph by John Starkie*

Ivy speaking to conference in Blackpool, 1976. Ivy remembers: "My mother had just died but we had to keep going as 2,000 delegates were there. My mother had helped me with the hymns for the conference service."

Ivy's last conference, Bournemouth 1977

Chapter Eleven

The Wind Beneath My Wings

After spending a quarter of a century as headmistress of Threshfield School, I retired in 1979. I had to wash the chalk from my hair and find a new life. I wasn't quite 60 but retired early because John had suffered a heart attack the year before.

I left behind a very different establishment from the one I had taken over. The roll had expanded to around 60 with a staff of three, including me, plus a part-timer. Tucked into our tiny stockroom with the telephone I also had the ultimate luxury of a school secretary, which was a huge help.

On my last day, we had a big luncheon party and I was presented with a mahogany desk which I treasure. The day passed in a whirlwind and the next morning we moved house, so I was too busy to become over-emotional about leaving, though I was deeply touched by the many good wishes I received. Looking at the log book containing comments by previous head teachers, I saw: "1900. School closed today for Queen's Birthday and The Relief of Mafeking." I couldn't beat that, could I?

We moved to Swindon, Wiltshire to be nearer Tim

Farewell party at Threshfield. Left to right: Mrs M. Pye, Ivy, Mrs S. Magill, Mrs D. Williamson

Right: Ivy's last Christmas concert, December 1979.

Below right: Ivy Starkie is presented with gifts on her retirement from Threshfield School after 25 years as headmistress. Left to right: Canon Barlow, Sgt Gains, who spoke on behalf of the parents, Ivy, A.L. (Tant) Dean, Chairman of the Managers, John Starkie, Ralph Billing, Area Education Officer.

and his family and before I had time to draw breath, I was embroiled in applying for a franchise to run the local radio station in Swindon, which took my mind off missing my former pupils.My daughter-in-law Maureen read in the local paper that people were being asked to get involved and, knowing my interest in public and community life, suggested I make contact. My experience must have impressed them, for once again I found myself working alongside some very interesting people, including Baron Joffe, who had been Nelson Mandela's lawyer, with whom I got on very well.

Johnny Morris, the zookeeper turned television star, was also involved and liked to sit next to me because we had a laugh together. He was just the same jovial person he was on the television. On the other side of the table was Pam Ayers, the poet. I wondered what I was doing there, for nobody had heard of me. It was a challenge but a welcome one and kept me on my toes. Sadly, after all our hard work, we didn't win the franchise. I was offered a job planning programmes for the group who did win but it would have been too far to travel.

Later, we moved house again, this time to Porlock in Somerset where for seven years I was a member of the Somerset Community Heath Council, an unpaid post working as a watchdog group for patients. To my initial dismay, I was allocated mental health services. At that time, they were closing the large hospitals which had started life as asylums. It was a huge mistake for 'care in the community', which was meant to replace them, left some vulnerable people alone and under-supervised.

At meetings with those running the health service, I would demand to know where patients had gone and if

*Tim and Maureen with their sons Stefan
and Andrew about 1981*

Tim   *Maureen*

they were being monitored. Often I would be told they were now living with relatives but I knew that in most cases that wasn't true for their families couldn't cope with them. Some doctors considered me a thorn in their side but it was my duty to stand up for those people with mental health problems who suffered severely as a result of this policy.

John's health was a constant worry to me for his early sufferings had taken their toll and at Bristol Royal Infirmary, John had heart surgery.

Afterwards, the consultant called me in and said I was not to treat John as if he was made of china but should encourage him back into reasonably active life. "There's something else I must ask you," he added. "How's your love life?"

I nearly fell off my chair. "It could be better," I replied.

"Wait until I get him in here," laughed the consultant, "I'll tell him."

What he was trying to say was that we should aim to return to normal life but it wasn't easy and I did worry but we managed.

Time seemed to pass very quickly after that. In the 1990s, John and I returned to the Ribble Valley where we found a penthouse flat from which in one direction we could see Pendle and the other Kemple End. John had come home, for he felt Lancashire to be so, and hoped to enjoy the last years of his life there. But it was not to be.

In 1997, one year short of our Golden Wedding anniversary, John died. At his funeral service in Whalley, the minister said, "His indomitable spirit kept him alive and he was a fighter to the end."

She detailed how much John had supported me in my professional and public life. He was "The wind beneath her wings" she said, and he was. I thought back to all he had been through, to the enormous strength of character which had taken him through unimaginable horrors. I considered myself lucky that fate had decided to bring this man who had lost everything into my life, for at the time I felt I had also lost so much.

In 1998 I moved to Cambridgeshire to be near Tim, Maureen and my grandsons Andrew and Stefan. I have had to pick myself up again and carry on. I'm getting good at that.

Tim with Stefan and Andrew, the men now in my life

Epilogue

I began this book as a tribute to the two very special men whom I have been lucky to have in my life. Somehow I have ended up writing quite a lot about myself but I'm glad to have recorded the solid and steady work done for the women's movement by those of us who felt much more comfortable wearing bras than burning them.

I hope it is also an interesting record of village school life from the 1940s to the 1970s. I have never regretted my choice of career, even if I had chalk in my hair every day of my working life. Sometimes, I think it is still there. I hope so.

There ends my romantic story, started on top of Pendle Hill. Philip said he would die (though not to me) but he would return and his spirit would be there on Old Pendle, which would always be there.

"We are such stuff as dreams are made on
and our little life is rounded in a sleep"

The Tempest, Shakespeare

John and Ivy Starkie after 25 years service with the B&P